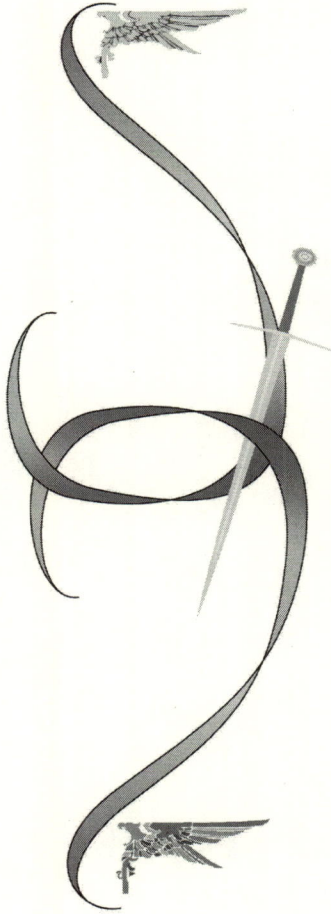

And Afterwards I will Pour Out My Spirit

© Copyright Sheri Hauser 2020
Published by Glorybound Publishing
Camp Verde, Arizona
SAN 256-4564
Printed in the United States of America
ISBN 9798580241098
Copyright data is available on file.
3nd Edition
Hauser, Sheri, 1957-
   And Afterwards I Will Pour Out My Spirit/Sheri Hauser
   Includes biographical reference.
1. Religious/Prayer.   2. Charismatic interest/Prophecy
I. Title

www.gloryboundpublishing.com

The Cover is from one of the Hubble Space Images.

Sheri's Dream Books

And Afterwards I will Pour Out My Spirit
Christian Authors Driving the Market
Dream Language Understood
Faith on a Wing and a Prayer
Filled with the Holy Spirit
Foundational Prophetic Prayer
Going to the Center of God's Heart
Growing Ministry to Seed instead of Fruit
Inspirational 3-D Poetry
Intimate Relationship with Jesus
Leading Prophetic Prayer
Living in the Haunted House of my Head
Living in the Shadow of the Sins of our Parents
Personal Prophetic Prayer
Preparing the Bride of Christ: Allegorical
Prophetic Interpretation of Art
Sharing Prophetic Gifts in the Church
Simple Fun Christian Dream Interpretation
Spiritual Authority Over Demon Dragons
Tactical Demonic Warfare
Why the Glory Departed

Outpouring of dreams, visions, prophecy and miracles
with Holy Spirit power.

And Afterwards I will Pour Out My Spirit

3nd Edition

Tomaseña

By
Sheri Hauser

Glorybound
Publishing

Glorybound Publishing
Camp Verde, Arizona
Released 2020

Greetings, in the love of God

Everyone has a desire to be happy. No one can truly be happy without God in the center of their being. This book gives ideas on reaching out and receiving from God. Sheri sees God demonstrate love, forgiveness, and mercy in her life.

Who is Sheri?
She is a gem with many facets: a worshiper of God, an ICU nurse, a mother, and one who speaks the truth. She is an obedient friend of God.

God has chosen her to lead others into this path. I am convinced that you will be touched in a new and profound way if you read this book with an open heart.

Who am I?
I have worked next to her and watched her grow in grace, mercy and in the gifts of the Holy God. I was there when she received the Holy Spirit. I have seen the changes in and around her life while she has prayed.

One of the greatest victories in prayer that I have had the privilege to join with her in, is with the rescue of her daughter, Joy, from drugs. For, when five of us joined with prayer and fasting, God worked the miracle of bringing her home. I am happy to say that she is now in college.

I am proud to say that Joy, her daughter, has asked me to become her God-father. It is an honor that I cherish. For, not only have I been able to see her become rescued from the grip of the enemy, but to grow up.

Who are you?
Someone who wants to know God better; one who is looking toward the dawn of God's manifested love, somebody who wants the Holy Spirit to show His power in their life. Your weight is over. Your wait is over. God will remove that burden from your heart.

Therefore, it is my honor to present to you this book. For, we all have some doubting Thomas in us, I know, because my name is Thomas.

I thank my God, always making mention of you in my prayers because I hear of your love and of your faith which you have toward the Lord Jesus and toward all the saints and I pray that the fellowship of your faith may become effective through the knowledge of every good thing which is in you for Christ's sake. (Philemon 4-6)

A brother in Christ,
Thomas McGlade

Thanksgiving

This book is not a book that could be written without being there. It is an account of experience, trusting that I heard God's voice clearly enough to do what He asked of me. This book started on the floor of a small church praying for the body of Christ. I wish to thank those who tolerated my growing pains and prayed with me. My daughter, Stephanie, has held my hand all the way. One of the most amazing things was how she grasped my hand and walked me straight into the arms of God. For the first venture at Church, we did together. It was to pass out bread to the poor. And, as I remember, we were too early, then. But, now, I think we are on time.

Brother Ron taught me that God is bigger than I think. Kris taught me how to be excited about Him. Rick taught me that I could be a professional and love God at the same time. Lana faithfully showed up and prayed with me for hours at a time. We prayed the entire floor of a Church, one square at a time. And Melinda, taught me to sing and pray at the same time. Thanks, Guys.

And, again, I would be remiss not to thank my husband, Paul, for enduring my night after night of jotting down the dreams. He is my best prayer support.

It is with thanksgiving in my heart to our Heavenly Father that I present to you Tomaseña. My prayer is that these words will motivate you to venture out, just like walking on water, and trust God to help move you from the doubts that you have into faith, trusting His voice is the one that you hear. May you be enabled, by His Holy Spirit, to deal with the Thomas in yourself, the Tomas-in-ya.

Chapters

Letter from the Author

Whatever you do, don't call me a writer. I'm not. The vehicle is not the destination. Writing has brought me to the destination, which is intimacy with my Lord. My goal has been to be like Moses and see the glory of God. As I have pursued Him, I wrote it down. Then, He told me to publish it.

He told me that the other day. So, I asked Him what I was? What do I call myself? He said I am the echo on the other side of the canyon. As He has spoken, I have echoed His voice. So, I give you these writings, my voice, His echo.

This is a collection of writings compiled from dreams, visions, and revelations. They provide a matrix for the training which I have received from the Holy Spirit. The teaching is from topical Bible studies. Much of what I have received, I got as I have spent a lot of time hiking in the desert outside of Las Vegas.

This is a picture book. It is word pictures. It takes hard issues of the Kingdom of God and presents them as pictures. They were given to me in pictures, and I share them the way they arrived.

There is an empty book on my night stand that He fills day and night. To me, the dreams are like gold threads coming down from heaven containing the voice of God. I try to catch as many as I can. I have accepted every dream as being a word from God and treat each with honor, bringing them all back to Him for help to understand them.

I asked Him once, "Why do you bring me these dreams like riddles? I have to work so hard to get them open."

He answered me, "Dreams are like boxes under the Christmas tree. Each one is a present from Me. Does a Father put all of the Christmas presents under the tree unwrapped? No, he wants to see the face light up when the gift is opened. I want to share the delight."

The start of it all happened when He gave me the same dream over and over. In this dream, I have a set of keys in my pocket that has been left by my father.

He doesn't need them anymore, so he left them for me. Since I have memorized a lot of Scripture, I knew the verses in the Bible on keys.

When God called them to my mind, I went to a friend who I knew had a close relationship with God. And, over some fried chicken, I asked him if it was possible that God could be talking to me in this dream. He was quick to affirm that God had spoken to a lot of other people in the Bible, why couldn't He talk to me as well?

So, I embarked on a study of the keys. I came across the most amazing verses in the Book of Revelation, which indicate that Jesus left us the keys to the Kingdom of God when He went to heaven. So, I asked God to tell me the answer.

Over the next three months, He gave me a dream about once a month. Each of those dreams brought me back to the same section of scripture. After that, I wrote down all of my dreams and began to see how they might be related to the Bible.

Because I didn't turn the light on when I wrote the dreams in the night, they were messy, so I found it hard to decipher in the morning. Consequently, I started typing them into the computer. Then, I would look in the Bible and pray for God to show me stuff. And, He did. I received incredible instruction, answers to questions, and guidance.

I developed a dream file over the next three years. It was for me. I never knew that others could do it. Then, I had a dream where God told me He wanted me to write a book. I was shocked. I had never written anything before, except in school, so I was terrified at the prospect of writing a book.

I decided to put it together three times, so I could be sure of how it went. I started compiling the dreams into organized files. After I spent a year putting the book together twice, I decided to fast. The third time I put it together, I fasted 40 days from bread and meat. I lost 20 pounds, and the dreams jumped to a new level. Whereas I had been having the picture type of dreams, I now began having word dreams. given to me in dreams and while I hiked in the desert. He has kept me on a specific time schedule.

The message that I have been given is that God wants to speak to They came like ticker tape messages in the night. I just copied the words. During the fast, I remember, one night, I became frustrated because I had little dreams. I would have a clip of about 10 minutes, wake up, write it down, then try to drift off to sleep. So, after an hour of this, I got up and sat in a chair downstairs. I figured that if I was quiet and stayed in the dark, I could continue to snooze, and the words might continue to come to me. They did. I stayed in that chair for several hours in the middle of the night. In the morning, when I typed the dreams into the computer, I had 9 typewritten pages.

So, I pressed God. I continued to fast another 20 days. During this time, the nighttime word dreams were pushed over into the day. Now, if I focus on listening to God's voice, His words will come to me. One of the most profound writings on Angels was written in the middle of a church service. (It's in Katisha).

The names, the outlines, and every detail for the books was given to me in dreams and while I hiked in the desert. He has kept me on a specific time schedule.

The message that I have been given is that God wants to speak to everyone. He wants to have an open path of communication with all of His children. These words were given to me. But, because He told me to, I now share them with you; because He told me that if I share them with you, you will reach out for Him... and He wants you to. I am a one topic person. I pray. And, I pray for you, as you read these writings, they will enrich your soul and encourage you to seek Him in a new way.   *God Bless, Sheri*

Speak to my heart. The heart will speak to the child in me.
Then I will understand. I sought heaven, and He
met me on earth. Be still and know
that I Am God. When you are still, and you
let Me talk to you. All will know Who I Am.
I own the quietness when I own you.
It's mine as you are Mine. Let's be Mine.

Greater Purpose

We dwell in a world full of menial tasks, longing
to recognize eternal purpose. Bombarded with
an overload of information that is useless, we
strive to make sense out of our lives. Since
He died, was buried and is risen, the
door has been
opened that provides
the light we need to
see greater purpose
in our lives.
He has
not
opened our eyes,
but
the
eyes of
our heart which
brings about an understanding
of the true meanings of life and purpose.

Amazing Grace

Be the one in a million who will carry His heart on a necklace
on the outside of your shirt. His heart over yours like His
face over yours. Be the one millionth
caller to win the free trips to Heaven's throne daily.
Open our eyes and look to the fields. They are white
for the harvest. It's not snow, it's little flowers. Little
dancing flowers. Smell. Amazing grace. Even I
notice. You hold the flowers that you didn't
grow.
You only
hold. I grew by My hand.
They are cut
but they continue to grow. Colors on
paper run when heated. Get the iron,
get the wax paper.
Heat and press. Beautiful
colors running together
to form a picture
that wasn't
planned
by you.
Press
it.
Pressed
flowers.
Spring flowers.
Delicate between
the layers of pages.
Behold the
love! Look. He's on the pages!
Fragrance and love, together mixed and
pressed. Turn it over. Page by page. Smell Him.

Open Door

Temporal identity is where we pick a job.
Eternal security is where
we find the long term investments

The Mystical Boat

The Dream*: He is unaccounted for. The boat came back, but it was empty. He was lost at sea, given up for dead. They had a funeral, buried the idea of His returning to land. He dropped down from heaven, but the boat is still there empty parked along the sea on the rocks.*

All the gear is there. Everything that they need to set out again. Nobody has used it pretty much since the boat came back. It just sits there empty, waiting for passengers. They're scared of the water, the sudden storms, and unpredictable winds. And, there is a funny feeling to use something that was used by someone so long ago, and now given up for dead.

They bury this stuff with Him, but it's not in the ground. It sits on the shore next to the sea, ready to launch out just like the day He left it there. It's our boat. He is the sailor lost at sea. He doesn't want us to use the boat to find Him, but to go to sea for ourselves. Catch stuff. There are places we need to go that have schools and schools of fish to be caught.

The water is teeming with life ready for the picking if we only use the boat to get there. Yet, we stand on the shore and look out to the sea. We think He will return to use His own boat. But, He has left it for us. If we put the boat into the water, it goes where He blows. He's the wind of direction that moves the boat. It is not a motorboat. There are no oars, but still, it goes to the right place. The mystical boat has a chain of gold when it's anchored in the safe -haven.

Interpretation:

Jesus used a boat 2000 years ago. He brought good news to those who were poor. He bound up the brokenhearted ones and freed those in bondage. He released them from sickness, emotional pain, and the power of death. He brought light into the dark places of our hearts to understand God in a way that was never possible before He came. He delivered everything that was needed to have complete victory over the Devil and his demons. And, He gave all these things to us through the Holy Spirit whom He sent to live within us. He has given us the same vehicle that He used. It is a boat that is along the sea on the rocks. When our spiritual eyes are open, and we see things the way He saw things, then we are 'by the sea'. The rock is supernatural insight that is given to us when we have an intimate relationship with God through Jesus Christ. When the relationship is built on His love, then there is a connection that is built between Him and us. He starts to whisper in our ear the secrets of His Kingdom.

The boat is the way. It is the vehicle that God gives us to get us to where we need to go. When we combine the Holy Spirit's power with the intimate relationship with God through Jesus, then we will find our boat; we will find our way. The dream says that everything we need is there.

All the tackle is still in the boat just as Jesus left it. God does not change, and the Word of God does not lie. Jesus has left us a complete package when He left us the Holy Spirit. All of the Holy Spirit has been given to us.

The boat sits empty, waiting for passengers.

Oh, to have those who hear the voice of God and walk into it with complete victory!

There are things that keep us from coming aboard that boat.

The dream says that we are scared of the water. Perhaps, we are frightened by the Holy Spirit. He is unpredictable. We do not have any control when we relinquish it to Him. When people speak in tongues, there is no control of the voice. The only control there is, is in the flow. The person can open his heart to allow the flow of the words to come through or not. And, the person has no control over the words.

The words are from God, totally. That is frightening to many. And, to them, it is frightening to think that the Holy Spirit might take them over. It is like entrusting the boat to the wind with the sails up and no motor. When the boat starts sailing, we no longer are able to control it alone. We need help. A sailboat cannot be sailed by only one person without great difficulty. But it can easily be sailed with two. Similarly, when we entrust our selves to the Holy Spirit flowing through us, He puts us into situations that we cannot control alone. We must rely on the grace of God to help us. This is frightening water to sail out onto.

Have we been taught that God moved through the hand of the disciples differently than He does now?

The teaching of the appropriation of the power of God moving through His people through being directed by His loving word has been given up for dead. It is a dead theology. Do we walk up to paralyzed people that lay by fountains, reach out our hands to expect them to begin to walk as if they were never paralyzed? I don't think so. We send them to surgeons and therapy. And we pray the way we have been taught to pray.

But, He says that He will lead us with His eye on us. When we allow Him to live within, we are merged with His thinking. As we start to think like He thinks, then we become the other eye in the I AM. We become His hands to fulfill His missions.

What are His missions? He has given us the boat to go to sea to catch stuff for ourselves He wants us to get a hold of all the victory that He has left us by His death, burial and resurrection. He wants to show us and enable us to receive that victory for others and ourselves.

He has schools of information for us. He wants to teach us about Himself. It is within the place of intimacy and flow of the Holy Spirit that we will find the wealth of knowledge, wisdom, understanding and counsel. And, He always empowers His word, so surely we will have the Spirit of Might flowing, as well. It is in this boat that we will see the miracles of God.

He longs to give life to the body of Christ. Not merely to live, but have life abundantly. If there is healing for us, we need to seek it actively through the direction of His voice and the power of the Holy Spirit.

He is the wind of direction that moves the boat. When we get into the place where the love of God is flowing through the Holy Spirit, His voice will be clear to us. He is the wind. He is the voice. He is the Word. Remember? In the beginning, was the Word and the word was with God and the Word was God. The same was in the beginning with God. The voice of God empowers us to move where He wills.

The chain of gold is the connection between Him and us. There is a bow that connects us to Him. We have a bond when we ask Him to become our Father and we become His child. We both commit to the relationship. A gold bond is formed. The bondage changes from that of the enemy to that of God. We do not have any choice. We are either under the kingdom of this world, Satan, or we choose to become part of the Kingdom of God. We become a slave to righteousness, rather than sin. We are no longer bound toward sinfulness, but rather, bound to do what is right according to the laws of God. The anchor is His heart. We become bound to His heart by the golden links of wisdom. This is our safe haven. We are put in a place like a safe haven protected from the enemy by the grace of God.

It is like a harbor to protect us from the tempest of the Devil. So, even if there is a mighty storm all around, we are safely in the harbor, because we have the bond to the anchor of His love, His heart.

Proverbs 1.9, 3, Isaiah 61, Mark 2.5, John 16.7-28, Acts 3.

Compass

When we are trying to get somewhere, we get into a car
and drive there. When God gives a vision, we need
to get into the vehicle that He provides and face
forward. Face Him. Facedown the road
that He sets before us. It is the road to
holiness through the cleansing
of the vision by His word
and His presence.
If we continue to seek His presence,
then He will keep us on the track. It is especially
important at the beginning of a plan. It is like a boat
starting out at one place seeking to sail to a selected
destination. If the compass is off by one degree, then
the boat will never end up at the desired place. It may
be close, but it will not be the true destination that
was planned on at the beginning. How does a
captain steer a ship? He does not rely upon
the first mate to tell him the reading
of the compass. No, He looks
at it himself. God has
provided us with
a compass.
He will
encompass us with Himself
when
we
go into
His presence
daily.
There, He will provide us
with His direction for the ship to
be able to reach the place across the sea.

Virgin Ears

Virgin ears have never heard. They are a closed
canal that has never been used before. A new
place. A potential to receive and conceive is,
then, waiting in the wings. Waiting for the
seed
and the
opportunity to enter, attach and grow.
God, please open our virgin ears
to receive Your word: Your
seed. Plant your seed
within our hearts
to
produce
ideas
after
Your
kind. Make
it ministry birthed by
God Himself. Father in us
Your seed. May our offspring be
Your wellspring. Grow within us new life.

Check In Closet

Everlasting righteousness is ours eternally
because Jesus bared His soul to the whole
world. He shared Himself. He opened up His
walk-in closet. The place where His garment
is kept. He unlocked the door and gave us
the key. Anyone may go to that closet.
It's a closet of prayer. And, ask Him
for something to wear. It's
like an eternal coat closet
when you pick up
your coat
after
a party.
We can
pick up our
coats from the
team
at the door. The
only difference
is we never checked
a coat in.
We didn't bring one. He just
provides. Righteousness freely given to
us one by one when we go to the check-in closet.

His Son

Seated at His right-hand in Glory
forevermore captured by His
love,
held within His hope,
between the hands
of time,
is His
glory
and
His
power
His might, His
magnificence, His Son.

Benevolent Benefactor
The mysterious one gives
to someone in dire need. The
needy one comes not knowing
that his
need has already been
met by another who passed on before
his time leaving an inheritance behind.
That's us. We have an inheritance that has
been left for us by a benevolent benefactor to
meet needs we don't even realize that we have.
His benevolence is a factor to our benefit. There is
retirement included in the benefits package, you know?

Seeing the Rocks

The Dream:

I am on the beach. I see some children who are drowning. They are trying to get out of the water by pushing against these big rocks. I can see from where I am that if they swim in a different direction, they will be able to go up on the beach without such a struggle. I go into the water after them and pull them out away from the rocks.

Interpretation:

God has given us the keys to the Kingdom of Heaven. He has given us the ability to pray with faith that removes mountains. When we see where we are going, we will have faith to be sure that is where we will end up. Often, we see situations as a huge pile of rocks in our way.

It is time to put on our bathing suits and go into the sea: the sea of knowledge, wisdom, and revelation. He will open our eyes to see the real mountains. These are not the visible ones, but the invisible ones; the spiritual mountains put there by the sea monster, Leviathan, the devil.

Often, when we swim, the water feels cold. Our emotions may be cold to what God wants us to do. We can't tell the seasons of God by feeling. Our emotions will not tell us what to do. We have to know in our hearts and believe the Word of God.

He wants to remove the mountains from our way. He has given us the authority to cast them a new role in our lives. The mountain melts when our spiritual eyes are opened to see the desires of the Kingdom of God in the situation. When we see them, we will become aware of them. We cannot deal with something that we cannot see. They are as piles of rocks placed there by the enemy. These are mountains of guilt, oppression, doubt, anxiety, dread, sickness, loneliness, etc. We should cast them out like Jesus cast demons out of those who were oppressed. God has already given us the authority to deal with them through the blood of Jesus Christ.

Often, we are pushing against visible mountains instead of invisible mountains. We try to find God with our brains. We will only get a headache pushing against things that are not meant to be moved. When our spiritual eyes are opened to see the invisible Kingdom of God, then we will not push against what He really desires for us, which is intimacy with our soul. Many times, we push against His plans for us, His desire for us, our need for Him, and the way we think things should be.

Attentive listening

Attentive listening is when we know what someone said because we were paying attention. There's a cost. Jesus paid the price for us and gave the Holy Spirit as our teacher. He talks, we listen. Be attentive. The cost was high.

Deep End of the Pool

Language is given to communicate a thought.
There is a difference between understanding the
language and understanding the thought. Why?
Because it is like a swimming pool. Not all of
us enter it from the same direction. It doesn't
mean we are shallow because we don't choose
to go deep with the ideas communicated to us
about God. It may mean we just never learned to swim.
I don't know anybody who taught themselves to swim.
Swimming has to be taught by someone who knows
how to swim and is not afraid to get into the pool
with us. God has given us the Spirit of Counsel
as our teacher. He is not one to hangout at the
deep end in the deep things of God, and yell
to us to swim to Him. No. He meets us where
we are and works with us every step of the
way. Before we know it, we will find
ourselves in the deep end of the pool of the
knowledge of God and wonder how we
Got there. Not alone, I guarantee that.
Unless we are different from any
body else I know. But, I doubt it.
Because, there is only one way
to the Knowledge of God
and it is through His
revelation to us of
who He is.
So, that
settles
that.
We all need a swim
instructor. When we ask,
He will give us a personal trainer;
a life guard to teach us about His ways.

Communion Bread

The Dream:
When I rescue my children, they will be as though they are drowning, yet I will come and save them. They will be brought through the sea by back floating toward the shore.

Interpretation:

As He opened the way for the Children of Israel to pass onto the dry ground, He brings us into a land of blessing. The children passed through the sea. Although that was a body of water, it represented God bringing about a supernatural deliverance by separating something that had never before been separated. The water parted as Moses raised his staff. The staff is also symbolic of bread. Just as Jesus is the bread of life, by His blood, we have communion with the Father.

Today, the sea will be opened for us if we raise our staff, our bread, to God. Communion with God through the Holy Spirit will be like raising our staff to God. It will cause us to see the things that are in the invisible Kingdom of God.

The Lord has opened the way for us to understand Him and His Kingdom. We must come near to Him and allow Him to awaken our hearts to hear Him call.

We need to be baptized into the sea (see). We must go from that place where we know we are blind to have our eyes opened. He will show us a whole new Kingdom.

The beach lays at the entrance to the sea (seeing what God wants us to do). He will give us knowledge and understanding that will flow up in us like streams. This is like the 'beach'. It is crushed rock. A beach is a place where the rock has been broken. It allows swimmers to have the footing to walk into their purpose. It is covered with white sand.

On the beach, the sands of time are all together in one place. He will tell us of His plans. God shows us the purpose of our lives from the front to the back of time if we ask.

He desires for us to back float, open our eyes to His purposes, lean back, and rest in Him. He will embrace us as we embrace the vision He has for us within the Kingdom.

When we stop trying to steer our own lives and allow the voice of God to direct us, He will lead us to a place of peace, bringing us the desires of our hearts.

Open Heavens

Behold, I have laid heaven's gate open for you. Just walk through it. Over the golden arches, golden bricks of wisdom laid on your heart. It is not a ticket to ride, but to walk into the Holy of Holies.

Thou Art Class

When I go to where You are. Thou Art. And
You come to where I am. Thou Art. You
are the teacher. The first and the last.
A one, above all. Yet You teach me.
Amazing. To be taught by You
The Thou Art Intuitive
Insubordination
When you just know
He's better than
you are.
He is.
God is
better than us.
His ideas are better.
His plans are better.
His vision is better.
How come we
still use
our own?
I don't think
I have much intuitive
Insubordination for this
aspect. I keep getting in the way.

Ministry

Dream:
When we rescue others, we both must face the sea. They cling to us, we cling to them and we both cling to Him. Together we swim for shore.

Interpretation:
We desire to share God with a world that is lost. The first thing that they see is not God, but us. Only, when they have embraced us, can we turn them around and point them in His direction for their lives. We cannot see their goals, they have not been given to us, but God will show them if we can get them pointed in the right direction.

To rescue others, they must look to the sea; they must see God for themselves. Our back needs to be toward the shore; shored up with the strength that comes through the power of the Holy Spirit. Our fleshly desires need to be put to sleep. We cannot work our way to heaven and should not teach others to do it. Our minds should be awakened along with our spirit to commune with God.

When we hear His voice to us, He will send us to do whatever job He has appointed us to do within the Kingdom of God. Every position within the Kingdom is used to remove the yoke of others and free them from the bondage of Satan.

The season has ended for us to focus on ourselves. We need to become more than a Church of 'one'. Just as there are five major bodies of water covering the earth, God has chosen five ministries to share the knowledge of Himself with the body. These are avenues to get the word out.

We need to empty our hands of the things that we hold dear and allow them to be filled with His purpose for the body of Christ. He will train us Himself. We need to get off the beach and get into the water and rescue some of the children that are drowning. It is selfishness that causes us not to go in after those who need us.

We need to extend ourselves for others, even though we may feel uncomfortable. We should take our orders from God, not others. He has a plan and, oftentimes, we do not understand when we talk to someone why we are doing it, but we have to open our mouths and trust Him to give us the message for them. We are the fire that brings the heat to a cool season.

Exodus 15:22, Psalms 48, Isaiah 11-15, Song of Song 4.15, Mark 1.16, John 21, I Corinthians 10.2, Revelation 4, 15.2.

Taught to Flow

The darkness has spilled over into the light. Be quiet. The flesh screams. Gag it with rag. The will jumps. Let the Holy Spirit teach you to flow from place to place walking on water. There is no other way to get there.

Reach Plant

The Lord wants to grow us Himself. He is the sun,
the water, and the air. For His Son opened the way
for Salvation. His seed was given to us. It is His
Son that has made the provision for our growth.
He sent us the water, the Holy Spirit. He is
within us, a well springing up to eternal life.
He brings eternal plans of God to life through
His power. The Lord provides the air. He is the
Voice of the one crying in the wilderness
for us to prepare our heart to receive His message.
In Him, we become grounded. Under His direction
we are led and into His throne room, we end up
in the end. He is the one, we reach for, by
His
provision
and His strength within.
We are like a tender plant-dependent
on the gardener to give us
what we need to grow
up into a strong
tree that
will
be
one
where
the birds can dwell.
Grow little plant, grow.
I will be the sun, water, and air.
I will be the ground and the sky. Just
reach, reach for Me. Reach for the vision.

God wants to Train His Way

Our Father wants to train us. God wants to build our training on an eternal track; His love. We cannot fit our old training from the world into the new place that God wants to give us for His Kingdom. God's training is moving. Things that He taught us several years ago were good for then, but now He wants to teach us something new. We need to be open to learn new things from Him. We have a new family.

We all need to be trained to hear God's voice. We can sacrifice ourselves for the service of God. Still, without His word of direction, there is no way to know whether the sacrifice was for others, ourselves, or God. The Church has gone through an extended period of self-denial. They are tired. They have given away themselves, hoping that they will receive a reward, but none has come. They have given up on getting any reward here on earth and think that the only reward will be in heaven. But they do not know how to let God examine their hearts and tell them whether or not the service was one that He wanted. They picked one that they thought God would like or one that someone else told them to do. God has been silent to them.

Some have given their tokens to pay others to do the work of God. They are hoping on the prayers and spiritual guidance of others to get them into right standing with God. Many have put their trust in their leaders just like a driver of a bus. They are hoping that the driver has read the map, will follow the signs of God, and collect enough tokens from them to get the (bus load) whole congregation into the place where God wants them.

We need to learn how to look out the front window to heaven for ourselves to see the road that God has for us. When we spend time in prayer and the presence of God, He will teach us His ways. He will teach us the difference between His Kingdom and the Kingdom of this world. We will learn about God when we put effort into it. He has a job for us and we need to ask Him about it.

God wants to move His people from the gifts of prophecy on to other gifts within the body. He wants to free us to become what He created us to be: When we learn how to hear His voice, then

He will lead us in other areas of ministry. We need to be put into motion.

The Holy Spirit tells us what to do and we must become obedient to it. There is a lab with this course. There is mental and physical discipline when learning from God. His words sometimes come in riddles.

Concerning the gifts, we, the students, should be like our Great Teacher if we are doing things right. We will learn and use them with the spirit of a servant. We must learn how to dispense that which is entrusted to us with meekness. God is calling us to become willing and obedient to follow Him. Growing into our spiritual gifting is our obedience demonstrated.

The unification of the Spirit is accomplished through the bond of peace; which is His peace to us, in us, and through us. God wants to train us to become peacekeepers not warriors. We need to stop fighting the Devil and declare the victory.

Psalms 68:18, Proverbs 22:6, Isaiah 2:4, 6:1, Micah 4:3,
Ephesians 4:8, I Timothy 4:7, Titus 2:4.

The Rising Son

Look, lift up your eyes
Revival is on the horizon. The Son rises again and again.
Let Jesus arise in your heart and shine in those dark places.
What manner of love the Father has bestowed on us that we
should be called the sons of the Most High God.
He is already seated.
We don't make Him rise, we just point Him out to others.
Declare Him to them. Revelation has come.
I will reveal Myself to My People.

Rising Love

When God gives His love to each of us,
it is not meant to be just for us alone.
His love is active. It is like yeast in
bread dough. If it is left unattended,
it will continue to rise and rise.
Yeast makes the dough to be alive.
The love of God is active and will
continue to rise within our souls.
It is only when we put ourselves
in a dark place that it is unable to
raise. We need to set the bowl
by the window of His light
and allow His heat to
warm our hearts.
Let His love
arise
within
us
to make us overflow
for
others
with the love that He
intended for us to have for them.

God's Heart Desire

From deep within, my spirit cries out. Deep without, He answers from His. He meets me at precisely the same level I am willing to go. It's not Him de throttling the relationship. It's me.

The Wilderness

Joseph was given dreams at the age of 17 that were meant not to be fulfilled for years later. They were very much real, and they were very much true. God began to give him the messages for his purpose in his life at a young age. He does the same for us.

The problem is that there is a space of time and training that happens between when God tells us the purpose, and it is fulfilled. Sometimes it is a short time, then, other times it is years before we walk into the 'promised land': that place where all of the promises are fulfilled. Many call that time of training, the wilderness. We need to take notes from some of the individuals in the Bible that were given promises, visions of the future by God, then rushed into them before they were trained. These ones tried to avoid the wilderness training, the SEAR School.

The military officers that become pilots all are required to go through SEAR School. It is a rigorous program where they take a company of men and put them in a simulated position of being in enemy territory behind enemy lines. They don't give them any food for the week. They receive coordinates on the map that will cause them to meet one another and ultimately lead to a place where they will be picked up if they can get there without being captured by the simulated 'enemy'. If they are captured by the 'enemy', then they are put in a mock prison camp. The men must learn how to work together through rough conditions to reach a goal.

God has a SEAR School for us that He puts us through before He sends us out into the area that He has planned. The SEAR School is not the goal and it is not meant to break the individual, but to make him tough when he gets into the 'real combat zone.' Whenever we pursue God's goals, the enemy will confront us at every turn. He will be there to rob and devour all he can, so God needs to prepare us to confront him.

The Children of Israel were prepared to fight during the time they spent in the wilderness. As they came out of the wilderness, they entered into battle after battle to conquer territory that God had given to them. It was easy. They never lost a soldier when they followed His instructions using the training that He had provided. Read it. Battle after battle the enemies are annihilated. Thousands of people were defeated, and the Children of Israel don't lose one soldier.

Back to Joseph. As soon as He received the dreams from God, He looked for their promises. When He had a dream that his brothers and his father were bowing down to him, He immediately told them. It was not the time for the fulfillment of that dream. No one but him could see it. So, his brothers became angry and jealous, and his father rebuked him and told him to shut up about his dreams. The dream was true, but the time of fulfillment was a long way off.

Abraham received a promise for a son who was going to become a mighty nation. He waited for, what He considered a reasonable time, and then moved toward the fulfillment of the words of God, himself. He took his wife's handmaiden and had sex with her. It was OK by the standards of that day, but according to the promise He had been given, it was wrong. He rushed into the promise creating disaster. God gave him Isaac at the right time. But by Abraham rushing into the promise of God, he created a whole other nation that was put at enmity with Isaac from the start. He caused a split in the plans. Like a fray in a rope. God had a plan to weave, but Abraham tried to connect his plan to Gods rather than follow it. It did not weaken the plan of God, but added another one causing a fray.

On the other hand, Mary, the mother of our Lord, received promises about Him before He was born. She is a beautiful example of what to do when we receive promises from angels. She prays them in. Notice what her response is to the angel when He tells her that she will be the mother of Jesus:

She says, "I am the Lord's servant. May it be to me according as you have said."

She responds with a prayer of obedience. She couples prayer into God's will with her obedience to become part of the plan. She reminds herself, and the angel, that she does not serve herself, as she lives, she serves the Lord. Then, she enacts the plan. She prays according to the plan that the angel gives her.

Wonderful! She is saying, "Hey, if God has a plan and He wants me to be part of it, count me in. And, by the way, because I know nothing in the Kingdom of God happens without prayer, I now pray to enact this plan.

I merge in unity with God to become part of the plan for His salvation of the world."

Then, further in Luke, when the magi show up and give their blessings to Jesus, she does not have a lot to say. The Scripture says that 'she held these promises in her heart waiting for their fulfillment.' May we follow the example of Mary. No wonder God chose her.

The wilderness is a place where we learn to depend on God for our needs. The Children of Israel were given bread for each day and parameters for living with Him and one another.

They were given guidelines for worshiping Him with sacrifices and shown how to become an organized nation.

When they entered the wilderness, they did not have a name. When they left the wilderness, they had a name; Israel. They became God's people there. He taught them who He was. He showed them how He could be whatever they needed. Their shoes never wore out, and sickness did not come to them. He became their total provision. They learned how to follow His presence demonstrated in the cloud by day and the pillar of fire by night.

If we truly desire to seek God's heart, we must go into the wilderness. We take the promises of God and allow Him to talk to us, train us and test us so that when we reach the time of the fulfillment of them, we will be ready.

My wilderness lasted five years. God gave me promises, visions, and dreams. And, like Joseph, I could not keep my mouth shut. It caused me problems among my family and friends. But, I knew that they were from God and that they were true. God provided me with a few faithful friends who believed that they were from Him. These encouraged me along the way. But, my main encouragement came from Him alone.

Early on, when I was rebuked by a well-meaning friend for interpreting a dream for a child, I cried out to God. I needed to be sure that I was on the right path. He responded to me with a dream. In the dream, I am in a car on the freeway to my Mother's house, who lives in Las Vegas. There is a huge billboard with a picture of me on it. There was a caption under it that said, "Dreams are for you."

After that billboard, there was another one. It was a picture of many people, a huge crowd. The caption under this billboard said, "Dreams are for them."

The interpretation of the dream was so obvious that I could not help but understand that God wanted me to continue down the road that He had put me on. My mother is with Jesus, having died from breast cancer a few years ago. So, the road is the freeway to the throne of God. On the road to the throne of God, dreams are huge signs for everyone, not just me.

When my friends and family called me crazy, God kept after me. So, I went to the desert. I took up hiking. The hikes got longer and longer. I found one with a cleft and went around and around that place. I encountered rattlesnakes, tarantulas, deer, a herd of long-horned sheep, and a full-size mountain lion.

God showed me His protection. At first, I would take my CD player with worship songs and sing to Him for half of the hike. Then, when I reached the peak, I would memorize whatever verse I brought. I would learn the verse as I walked through the cleft part of the hike.

He started to talk back. I would bring an index card and write down what He told me. I called them diamonds. I knew that they were part of the diamond-tipped sword that He was putting into my hand. The paper has grown. One card turned into two. Now, I bring a notebook. I have so much scripture memorized that He, now, calls to my mind what He wants to shine His light on.

Let me encourage you, friend, that if God has put a vision into your heart, to treasure that vision. Try not to worry about what others think. God will not give you anyone to follow if the vision is from Him because He wants to be your teacher. He wants to take you up a trail that has not been hiked before. Press Him for the answers on how to get there.

Be like Mary. Voice your obedience to the plan, pray into it, and look toward its fulfillment. Then, like Mary, you will also birth God's word in your life. You will birth His vision, His plan, His baby. I know. I have.

And don't be afraid to ask Him for a new name. Abram, Sari, and Cephas all received a new name along with their promises. I ask because He says that we don't have because we don't ask. So, don't be afraid to ask. I do.

My latest new name is Lacy. He gave me this name because He told me that I am like a lace curtain, a veil. I see Him, then, show my view of Him to others in a fancy way, like a lace curtain. Let me encourage you to ask for a new name. I believe He has one waiting for each of His children.

Exodus, Luke 1.38, 1.80, 2.19

His Desire

You can feel the power as God works through His people to make them become His desire. As our desire is for Him, He fulfills our desire. His desire is for us, we fulfill it.

Call to Me

People don't understand the many ways you can call out
to Me. Not only can you call out with your lips. You
can call with your heart, your soul, your life. When
you yearn, you reach toward My Spirit. They
are all reaching for Me. It is like they are
pulling at a line. Then, all of a sudden are
surprised when a colossal Sailfish surfaces.
You tug at My heart, but are surprised
when I show up. The line has brought
the Presence. The promise is, ' call to
Me, and I will answer you.' When
your heart calls to Me, that
is how I respond: with
My heart. When
You call
with
your being,
your whole self,
guess what? The whole of Me shows up.
That's How
you come
to know
the
Seven Spirits.
It's the heart yearn that
moves you into this place with God.
Come to Me for the keys. If you want to take
a tour of the mansion beforehand, just go ahead.

No Met Yes

Life is full of negatives.
Just because something is negative,
doesn't mean we should not go there.
Don't, not now, no
I won't go
I'm not ready
Not prepared, unfit
Not dressed, behind the power
curve and not able to keep up.
I can't do it alone.
Don't go there
No, not now.
I won't
No can do.
Nothing
doing,
I'm not ready.
But, low met high.
Low met the Highest on the
rock in the ocean by the sea.

Porch Light

Light of my day, come light my night.
Night be bright, bring insight.
Oh, wings of the Dove, descend on me, I pray.
Bring hope, healing, and heaven.
I open my door, stand
on my porch,
extend my arms, and open my heart.
Come fill my spirit, flood my soul,
bring Your Dove, love, light.
Oh, glorious Holy Spirit,
I need supernatural input: Surges
of Your power, pulsating through my being.
I rely on You to help me stay on the porch
and not run for cover into the darkness of my house.
Plant my feet in Your love.
Brace me with Your statutes
and gird me with understanding.
Whether I sit, stand, kneel, or be on my face;
Help me, Dear Lord, just to stay and not run.
Teach me to fear only You;
To put away the fear of my sin, fear of others,
fear of me and learn Yours.

Fellow Climber

We need to view our training in the wilderness as an adventure
into the secret things of God. It is a mountain climb on a new
trail. We will see things never before noted by human eyes.
We will hear the voice of God telling us things He has not
said to anyone before. We will learn to have Him as our
climbing partner. Let Him pound in the nails into the
rock. We learn to trust. Then we must learn to grab
onto the ropes that He throws down to us.
It takes discipline to climb a mountain.
Discipline and strength.
The mountain usually gets steeper
toward the top. But, by the time we reach
the top, we are generally in pretty good shape.
As we near the top of the vision that He has for us,
we come to the place where we can feel the victory.
The wind is in our face. Our face glows with His
reflection. The sun rises in our face. What fun
it is to watch it rise. We are the ones who
have climbed that mountain
and now can see the
whole place
that we
have
come
from...
and then
the sun rises
to give a golden
glow to the whole picture.
He instills the power through
the blood of His
Son to the vision. The Precipice. The infusion
of Might pushes the vision to the top. Praise God!

The Climb

When you are obedient to the vision that God
has put in your heart. Then you can say that
'You gave it your all' so they can say
'thanks'.
The mountain climb will be worth the
effort when you reach the peak
and
lookout on all
that God has given you.
Become a mountain
climber
for
Him.
Climb to
that place within
His presence
that reaches
to the
height
of His vision.
Your Bus
Let your bus edge up
the mountain
on the windy road God has for it. It
stops every few miles so the engine won't
overheat. It is just getting close to the fire of God

A Bear

The bear sleeps in the cool of the
winter and arises in the spring, hungry.
The sleeping bear is awakened from a
long season of hibernation. Awakened to
feed off of things in the forest. He does not
eat people, He eats anything God provides;
ripe fruit and meat. Awakened by the Word
of God, God has sent an earthquake to awaken
a hunger; a season of growth, consuming fruits
and foraging in the bushes for His provisions
within the forest. What was hidden is now
being awakened. It is the season. The
summer is now. Turning on
the light of the
knowledge
of
God
into
the hearts of men.
It is an awareness
of His presence among them.

Famine of the Words of God

Prophecy has entered the bedroom:
I have removed the door.

Foretelling and forth telling the Word of God providing direction and encouragement to His people has entered where the Church sleeps. Prophecy has come to awaken it. To remove the door, it must be taken off the hinges. God is using us as tools, not just to open the door, but to remove it forever.

The Dream

I am in a mudroom of a house (ante-room where you remove your boots before entering the house). The door is open, and a large beautiful blackbird flies into the room. It is a tropical bird with shiny feathers and a crimson ring around its eye. It talks to me. It has flown in through the garage because the door is open.

I follow the bird out into the garage. It takes the garage door opener and hides it up in the rafters out of my reach. Then, it shows me some caged birds. As I look at the caged birds, I notice two green parrots who have only known captivity and two beautiful blue baby birds who have been caught and put into the cage.

The bluebirds are sad and look like they are about to die. They are walking amidst the droppings in the bottom of the cage. As I pick up the cage under the instruction of the blackbird, there is no back to the cage at all. Once the cage is picked up, the birds could fly free.

He tells me to let the bluebirds go free and to place the parrots in with the puppies who are caged in the garage. There are four puppies, as there were four birds. They are in a cage in the center of the garage. This cage does not have any walls, but the puppies are staying in.

Interpretation:

The blackbird symbolizes God's words carried through His messenger service on the wind (the Holy Spirit). It often comes through the darkness in the form of the gift of dreams at night. The red circle around the eye gives special attention to the vision, which is encircled by the representation of the blood of Jesus. The blood of Jesus Christ encircles the vision of the words for His people.

The messenger finds me in the ante-room with my shoes removed as I realize that going into the dwelling place of God (the presence of His Holiness) requires cleansing. The bird is a tame bird that has been taught to say only what the master wants it to say. God's vision for us is to be totally free as He takes the garage door opener and moves it out of the way. A garage is a place where things are stored for the 'next season'. As God has taken me to the garage, He makes me aware that the 'tools of God' need to be taken out at their seasons. We have stored them rather than listen and be aware of when God wants to use His tools in His Kingdom. He longs to build a Kingdom. The caged birds are innocent truths that God has provided for His people. Rather than building a nest for them, they have put them in storage. The cage is of deception built by the enemy. Thinking we need to 'save things for a different season.'

The cage is a weaving of deceit by the enemy to which we are being held in captivity. Waywardness and complacency caused by our stubbornness and rebellious heart have caused us to turn from having God being in charge of our lives. We have permitted our Church to be taken captive by Satan. We have listened to false prophecy because it has allowed us to be complacent.

We haven't given to the true needs of the people. We have taught them to be religious. The true needs are companionship with God and nurturing by the Divine Shepherd.

We need to release prayer and praise within the Church. The birds are representative of prayer...the ones on the floor that are blue...and praise...the parrots that sing all the time, even when caged. There are two of each because they are called to reproduce. God is always interested in having spiritual children.

The puppies represent companionship with the master. We need to take them out of storage and bring it into the bedroom. The bird tells me to allow the parrots to join the puppies and to release the bluebirds. Prayer would be released, and praise would become joined with companionship with Our Shepherd. All need to be taken out of the garage because it is the season.

The promises of God have been paraphrased by those put in charge of the house. There is deceit of humanism and flesh. They are for self-gain and spend more time placating each other than caring for the needs of the people. They have caged the birds and the puppies. They have put them into storage, and are killing them. They have thrown prayer, praise and intimacy with the master out of the house. They do not clean the cages, even.

The teachings are not pure but have their own sweepings mixed in. There are those who sicken, rather than release the newborns. There are those who do not preach from a pure heart, yet, expect loyalty and following. They sell the sweepings with the wheat. Gossip and smut with the words of the Lord.

The word of God is no longer coming in through the front door, He has removed the garage door by opening it permanently. He will swoop in with dreams of the night and speak to His people, Himself. It has become a door that cannot be closed. His desire is for this to be a season of praise, intimacy and prophecy brought into the Church through cleansing. To enter the house in the dream, one must go through the ante-room, remove your boots and wash up.

There is a time of purification that is needed for the house and, it's coming in through the back door. There has been a famine of hearing the words of the Lord, but now is the season to remove the tools that we have put into storage and learn to listen to His voice.

Psalms 104, Proverbs 1, 6.1-5, 26.2, Ecclesiastes 12.1-14, Isaiah 31.5, Jeremiah 12, Lamentations 2, Hosea 11, Amos, Matthew 8.20, 13, Luke 9.58, Romans 1.18, Revelation 18.

Sing Soul

Sing, soul,
sing for His love is eternal.
Hallelujah! Let my praise ring!
Sing, heart, sing,
overflow,
spill out.
Let that fill the air.
Nothing can tame a soul in love
with Him. The passion is from the
eternal one the lover of her
soul. And He just feeds
it with His own
passionate
love.

In Tune

We are like the children in a car. We each want to listen to our own station; the one we are tuned into. Ask Him to attune us to His station. Be reprogrammed, to become returned, to get in tune.

Death and Life

The winds of time blow with the current God provides.
It shouldn't be odd that He can do what He likes with
it. Each of us has kissed death and passed on. Just
like a man kissing his wife on the cheek on his
way to work. Some kiss more than others.
We go cheek to cheek with danger barely
recognizing it's implications. For many,
the closest we feel we have come to death is at birth.
Our first gasp of air was a tremendous relief to the ones who
nurtured us for nine months. There is a change. Our lungs
need to learn to breath with the air. What if it does not work?
Death catches up with us before we are born. So, death
becomes a failure to breath on our own. A break
from reliance on others to provide
our nutrition. The cord has not been
cut when it needed to be. At some point
we need to stop relying on what others
tell us. There's a critical point in our
lives when we should be
born.
We need to
be released from
the umbilical
cord and
breath
on
our own.
Seek our own
view of God, our own ideas
from Him. Take in His air and His
oxygen. Bond with Him. Find newness of life.

Bypass Surgery

Here's a pair of dreams with the same title:

Dream:
God says, "The Church needs a bypass."
I ask God, "Where is the problem?"
His response is, "It's with the upright. They need to answer the call. I am calling My church. She has to see where she needs to go and walk into it like a toddler.""

Interpretation:
God is like a father coaxing His child across the room to walk. He wants to teach us to walk His direction, listening to His voice. We have no idea how or where others should walk. That is why it is important to teach them how to hear God's voice for themselves.

It's like the babies are born, and we are stealing them from God. We are getting in the way, having them follow us instead of Him. It is like that guy that taught geese to follow His yellow boots rather than their mother. They bonded with the first thing that they saw. He wanted to do an experiment, so He practiced until He got it down.

We have done the same thing with our new believers. We have put on our own 'yellow boots' and told them to follow us. Just like a scientist, we cannot teach them how to gather food or fly. We do not know what they need because we are not their real parents. They have been born into the Kingdom of God, and have become Children of His. He is their Father.

When we try to raise young Christians ourselves, it is like trying to raise geese. We have no idea what they need. God has a special instructional package set aside for them, of which we know nothing about.

Perhaps He wants to raise them up to write books. If our gifts are in the area of singing, we will direct them toward our gifting, and it will be way off base.

They will be frustrated and stop. Also, God speaks the languages of the heart. Our hearts all speak different languages, just like 'tongues' are different languages. He knows how to respond to each of us individually with His language. He cuts through all of the interpretation problems. No one else will ever understand us like God.

Here's the second dream:

I am at home. There is a patient upstairs that has had heart surgery. He is staying in my study. I hear a knock at the door, then it opens. The person is used to coming over to my house. A heart surgeon enters to make a house call. He is quickly followed by a lung doctor. They have come to check on their patient. They find him in good condition. He is discharged.

Interpretation:

This patient is in my study, so I think He is me. God has repaired the flow of His heart to mine. I needed blood flow and oxygen to my heart and lungs. I have been having heart pains and God has come to repair my problems.

He has come as a heart surgeon and lung doctor to my house. His voice was not getting to the heart of what matters most in my life. I was not connected to His heart. He has repaired the flow of His heart to my body. Me. His word is the oxygen that I need to survive. With His word, I have a new life; I am born again. His word needs to flow throughout my spirit to give me the ability to walk in that new life. His voice has healed me. He has repaired the obstructions that were in my heart.

I have taken in harmful things that have scarred my heart, causing me to not be able to experience the joy of the Holy Spirit flowing through my spirit. I had built up scar tissue. He has performed a bypass on me. In the same way, He wants to perform a bypass on His Church. He wants the flow of blood and oxygen to come freely to His body. Some individuals are impeding the flow. They are blocking the system.

I was one of those. I had developed 'rote' methods of prayers and teachings. These papers clog up the flow; interrupt God's voice to others. May He help us when we interrupt His voice as He tries to speak.

In the dream, the physicians walk in through an unlocked door. We must unlock the door to our hearts and allow God to send us healing. Only open hearts can receive healing because it must come through the door. He won't come through walls, and He doesn't jump over gates. But, as often as we call on Him, the great physician will make house calls. He will come with His voice (air) and His blood (forgiveness) to give us healing and direction.

Altar Of Your Heart

Intentions meet provision at the purpose.
Purpose and provision meet intention and
obedience at the altar of your heart.

Seasonal Unity

Where is the unity of the brethren? In the cistern.
Because, when you fill me and I fill you, who will
fill us both? The Spirit of the Lamb lives to fill.
But, the cups are fractured and cracked. Let the
cups be cleared. For, when they are in the
hand of the One who washes, He repairs
the places of brokenness in us. The
Holy Spirit is the one who clears the
table making way for our cleansing
through Jesus Christ.
But our sink
is broken, too.
The water has been
turned off. We think
the bill hasn't been
paid, and we
keep
calling the
power company.
But, that's not the problem.
It was paid at
Calvary.
The pipes have
frozen. We haven't cared
for the season. They should have
been wrapped; blanketed in His love.

Seek Him

Why is it that we seek help from everybody else, and go
to the Father last? It is His plan that we come to Him first.
It will avoid all that stumbling around as we follow advice
that is not meant for us. He has the blueprints in His
hand and is the One who will read them to us. *He has
not given any other person the blueprint of your life.*
They only know of their own lives
and the evidence of God's hand in the lives
of others. They can give advice on how others
build their houses. But that house is not ours.
The ground and the building products
are not the same. And the purpose
will be different. Only God
can build a house
in the desert
to be used
in the
city.
I want to be the
whisper in the
wind on the other side, abundantly.
Call Me
*I have given you free access to all the money in
Heaven and earth. I have an access number. Call Me.*

Heart Surgery

Dream:

My Stepfather needed heart surgery. He flew in. He was late. I was getting dressed and unable to get a hold of him to pick him up. The Anesthesiologist decided to pick him up. He knew the way. I was getting ready before He came. I was putting on underclothes. They were closing down the OR. He was to be the last case. I was to be part of the surgical team.

Interpretation:

My step-father is God. He had become my step-father when I became His adopted child. The dream says that He needs heart surgery. Heart surgery is to repair clogs in the arteries that supply oxygen to the vital organ that pumps blood to the rest of the body. Usually, we need heart surgery because there is a build-up of plaque in an area resulting in a clog. God is saying that He wants to go around those clogged areas of our lives and restore the flow to us. The blood flows from the heart.

The blood of Jesus flows from the heart of God because it was His love to us that sent Jesus to die for our sins. We need to call this to remembrance and restore the flow of that forgiveness on a daily basis in our lives.

He flies in because He is a dove. The healing comes on the wings of the dove. He flies to us when we need Him.

The anesthesiologist is the Holy Spirit. He is the one who interprets the voice of God for us. He picks up on His voice and brings it to us. He knows the way to God.

In the dream, I am putting on my underclothes. I need to adorn myself in the righteousness of Jesus to be ready to meet the Father through the Holy Spirit. When I ask forgiveness for my sins and seek cleansing, then I am becoming adorned with His righteousness; I have put on my underclothes.

There are things that block the flow of all that God has for us to the body, the Church. There are those who claim His glory for themselves.

They are standing in the way of the Holy Spirit's voice being delivered to the body of Christ. These leaders are making their bank accounts fat at other's expense. They are clogging up God's flow to the body, snatching all of the fat food for themselves.

Perhaps we are the ones standing in the way from the voice of the Holy Spirit getting to us. If we have been taught that God only speaks through certain individuals, then we will refuse to listen to His voice. We have become the block ourselves. The message of the dream is that God is going to clear out the blocks. He wants His love and forgiveness to flow freely from His heart to His body, whether it be the body of Christ as a Church or us individually. For, we are the temple of Christ.

The OR will close down after Jesus opens up the flow to the body of Christ. He will have the last word.

Father, please give us open ears to hear Your voice. Help us not to be a block in your body that rejects the flow from Your heart to your people. Amen

Sand Bar

You put only good stuff in, but bad stuff comes
out. What happened? There was old stuff caught
in the middle. Allow God to take you back over
your life to the places where it came in. Cleanse
and heal. Kick it out. You have authority as
a child of God to be free from all evil.
In and out. Don't put up with it.
Nothing can change the sands
of time. But, He can move
it from our beach to His.
He sees the changes
that need to be made.
Let Him. We have
to meet Him
at the sea
with
our sand.
It's our sand bar.
It's what keeps us back
from launching
that
boat
into
the
ocean;
launching
that ministry
into His place. He will
wash that bar away and replace it
with His healing. Himself. We will see
what He sees. The bar will be made sea.

Cardiac Tamponade

Dream:

God has a cardiac tamponade. His heart overflows with extra blood. He is bursting to overflowing. We have not used the blood He has available to us from His heart to wash us of our sins. So His heart continues to be crushed from the pressure in His chest, pressing down on Him. It's so heavy. Relieve God of His heavy heart. Come to Him. Claim His blood for everything in your life and claim the treasure chest He has for you. Things He wants to share that are on His heart. He's pressed. He wants to overflow us. To share Himself, His goodness.

Interpretation:

God is interested in the attitude of our hearts toward Him. He does not read our lips, but our hearts when we pray.

I realized this when I was taking care of a very sick man on a respirator. Through the night, He had gotten a little better. In the morning, his elderly wife came into the room. She was hanging on tightly to a rosary. I told her that her husband was better. She replied, "Thank You, Sweet Jesus."

Then she turned to me and said, "I have been up all night praying the rosary for him."

Anyone familiar with the rosary prayers realizes that they are repetitious prayers that follow the beads around the rosary. She had spent the entire night saying repetitive prayers around the beads. She had not said a prayer of healing for her husband. But, she did. Her lips were saying the standard rosary prayers, but her heart was crying out to God all night on behalf of her husband. God heard her heart cry, not the prayer of her lips.

God sees hearts that are open to Him. He responds to them with His heart. When we talk with God, it is our spirit responding to His Holy Spirit that gets the message across to Him. We come through the blood of Jesus, as it is Him that brings our messages to the throne of God.

So, we pray with our hearts through the blood of Jesus' spirit to

59

Spirit. Our lips don't have to move for us to pray.

God wants more than anything to be with us. He has taken down every barrier that prevents us from coming to Him. If we feel that there are barriers between Him and us, then they are on our side of the fence. Song of Solomon describes us as a garden. There is a fence around our garden with a gate. The gate can only be opened from the inside. Our world, us, in the garden. We must open ourselves up to Him from the inside. He will not pry open the gate, and He does not go over the fence. We build walls to keep Him out. There are areas in our lives that we have closed off to him. We have posted 'Keep Out' signs. Those closest to us know which topics we won't discuss. They are the 'sensitive' ones that trigger bad emotions.

These secret gardens are the places that God wants to visit. Each time we open up another area of our life to Him, then we have torn down one of those 'keep out' signs and allowed Him to enter that place.

When we feel out of touch with God, then we are. We must allow Him to examine our hearts to tell us where the block is. We will find that we have secretly built a block wall that has prevented Him from coming into that area. Getting close to Him is a continual process of giving over areas of our lives to Him. It's not about Him controlling us. We are controlled when we are not under His supervision. He is the only one who knows the condition of our hearts. If there are problems with us, if we are sick in the heart, we will not know it unless we ask Him.

We do not have a microscope to tell if we have cancer sneaking up on us at the cellular level. In the same way, we do not have the insight to know if sin is sneaking up on us. As long as we are in the flesh, living in the world, sin will sneak up on us. The cancer cells will invade us regularly. Greed, selfishness, envy, lust, hate, and all of those sins that are always around us will sneak in unless we post a guard to our heart.

When we turn over areas of our lives to the control of Jesus, then He becomes the watchman for us. For example, if we turn over the area of 'what we see' to Him, then He will help us to not watch harmful programs on television. He will protect us from wandering into sin unexpectedly.

About five years ago, I came back to God after marching on my own for 10 years. When I came back to Him, I went to the desert and had a talk with Him. I was brutally honest. I told Him that I did not love Him, and had been lying to Him when I told Him that I did in my earlier Christian years. I told Him that I refused to sing any more 'love songs' to Him because it would be lying. I did not want to live the lie anymore.

Then, I challenged Him, "God, if it's possible, teach me to love You."

I am sure that is the most powerful prayer that I have ever prayed. We do not have what it takes to love God. If we try to love Him with our own love, it is too flimsy for the relationship and will not hold out. But, if we give up and turn over the whole program to Him, then He will take it. I allowed Him to come inside me and give me His love through the Holy Spirit to enable me to love Him. That is trading in temporal love for eternal love.

Whatever is on our heart, He already knows it. He knows the words before they are on our lips. One of my favorite sayings is that there is always room at the foot of the cross. We are all sinners and equally in need of His forgiveness and how I thank Him for saving a spot on the grass for me when I need it.

Deut. 4.29, Psalms 57.15, Isaiah 59.1-2, Romans 8.38-39.

UV

Filtered light takes out the harmful Ultraviolet
Rays. I have filtered out My judgment for
your sins. It is a red light. Like a
Christmas light bulb. My
light leaves you
with only the
true light.
Day and
night.

Strawberry Love

Your love exceeds our emotions. Up and over, around
and through, Your love flows. On the mountains
and through the woods. When we're in the
most intimate prayer and when we are
caught in the thicket. It permeates
to the smallest details of our life. He does
things, then waits for us to notice. He grows wild
strawberries
along the hiking trail for us to much on as we go along.
Do we consider how that little plant was started a few
years back. How He tenderly blew the seed and placed
it along the trail of your life's walk. Then He provided
the exact amount of rain and sun to make it grow into
maturity. When it was plump and red, we walked
by and popped it into our mouth. We savored
the flavor, delighted in the sweetness
that He had prepared way in
advance.
He was waiting for us
to come that way.
Imagine how
He feels
when
we
pop
that
berry into our mouth
and say,
"Thank you, Jesus."
I think it brings wetness to His eyes.

Filling the Need

God lives to exalt His Word. His Word lives within.
He lives to exalt us.

The Church is a Bank

Dream:
   *The scene unfolds in a bank. There are several church members
with me being held captive in the lobby. It is our own community
bank. We actually own the bank because everything we have is
invested in it. But, the bank is run by someone else. Although we
should know that we own it, we are acting like customers instead
of ones that do the service for others.*
   *As we come in to make withdraws, we enter into a hostage situa-
tion. They round us up and hold us at gunpoint in the lobby. They
don't seem to be too interested in taking the money, but in keeping
us from doing it.*
   *The guards don't abuse us but merely contain us. We realize that
if we do not get out, we will be killed.*
   *As a group, we start to come up with ideas on how to get out of
the situation that we are in. One of my friends has a cell telephone
and calls her husband to tell him that we are in the bank and need
out. He says that he will send someone to help.*
   *Someone else has a pocket flashlight. He goes to the window and
attempts to make signals out the window to a passer-by so that
he might see that we need a rescue. But, it was light outside, and
no one could see our light. We all knew that we would be killed,
eventually.*
   Then, another friend turns to me and says, "Why don't we get on

the floor in a circle and pray?"

I say, "How embarrassing! To kneel on the floor in front of the robbers would be putting us at risk. They might shoot us in the back as we pray. Besides, I don't think the situation is that urgent."

Interpretation:

This is a great dream with a lot of meanings. I have learned a lot from it, that is why I will share it with you.

The bank can either be the Church, or the vault of God. I think it represents both. If we use the analogy of the bank being the Church, then the lesson is that we are responding to our Church like it is a bank.

Perhaps, we put everything we have into it, yet do not consider it ours. We have not accepted ownership of it. We assume it is part of the community structure of God's Kingdom. With this analogy, we go there giving of ourselves and expect that we can make withdraws based on our account. If we have invested a lot, then we expect that it will be there for us when we need it. To us, the drive-through should have extended hours if we have been working in the front office on our days off. In contrast, we think others who only give a little, should only expect a little in return.

The church becomes a give and take environment. The ones that make larger donations receive the better seats in the sanctuary and the more beautiful envelopes to put their money into. Maybe, we trade recognition for service, making sure to recognize those who contribute more to a project, a program, or a building fund.

The message of the dream is that we are held captive by these ideas. The question that I needed to answer when I worked on the interpretation was, "Who are the robbers?"

The question is, "What is keeping us captive within our Church? If we have invested, why is the enemy able to keep us from withdrawing the riches of it? Who is the enemy?"

The second analogy to the bank is the storehouse of God. He has riches held in store for all of us. There is a bank vault full of blessings that waits for us to come in and make withdraws. So, if the bank represents the place where the blessings of God are stored, then why are we in a hostage situation? In the dream, all of us come to make withdraws, yet none of us goes home with any. We get delayed and held at gunpoint, thinking that we will die. In the dream, the enemy isn't frightful but controlling. He isn't mean, but determined. And, he has the upper hand because he is pointing his weapon at us and we are frightened of it. A crucial question is: Who is the enemy?

I believe that the enemy is revealed in the last part of the dream. Remember, the first person uses a cell phone to call her family for help. When we want something, do we ask others, rather than God? Who is our provider? Do we come to His bank, then ask the person next to us for a loan?

The second person uses a pocket flashlight to signal out the window. He uses his light to shine through the window.

God has provided us a window to see His wisdom in situations for our lives. The widow is our heart. He speaks to our hearts, then our hearts must speak to our mind before we can understand what He is trying to say to us. If we try to use our own light, we will never find Him. We will never be rescued by using our own ideas on how to find God. Our own ideas will not bring us relief from the prison situation. It is light outside, and the person shines their light out into the daylight. All of us are the same. None of us has any more insight into the things of God than the other. God is the one who provides insight. If God is consistent, then it is not the man, but God that brings the solutions to us. We will not find better solutions by going to someone 'more spiritual'. If the solution comes from God, the only difference in how much a person knows of Him is how open he is to God's voice. We all have an equal opportunity to be open to hearing God's voice. Education does not make us hear God better. Being a Christian for 20 years rather than 20 minutes does not make us hear Him better, either. What makes us hear Him better is listening more attentively.

The third person in the dream comes to me, asking if we should pray. My reasons for not praying are pride, fear, and wrong perspective. I do not think that the situation is serious enough to spend time on my knees. My vision is blinded. Amazingly, we are faced with death, yet, I do not see the situation as dangerous.

My second problem is fear. I am afraid of being shot down by the enemy. Are we afraid to call a prayer meeting for fear we will be shot down? The message of the dream is that when we face God and turn our back on the enemy, then we will find victory. Victory is found on our knees together as a Church.

If we are complacent in our situations of bondage, then the enemy will continue to hold us there. We will never be able to use the riches that God has to offer us. Prayer releases the riches of God for our personal lives and for our Churches.

Another message of the dream is that our prayer needs to be sincere and reverent. We need to spend serious time on our knees, all at the same level, on the floor, in the lobby. We are facing death, yet do not see it as serious. Our families are dying of sin and sickness, yet we are too proud to get on our knees, asking God to save them.

I find that when I pray if I get on my knees or my face, I get twice as much done in half the time because God quickly reveals my own sins to me. Then, I confess my sins and am able to pray for others. Because, you know, it does no good to pray when you have sin hanging over your head? So, I remove my sins first, then, I go onto whatever is on the agenda.

Being on the floor in a circle makes none better than the other, and God is the leader. With Him as lead certainly there will be victory

Numbers 23.19, Jeremiah 7, 23.24, Hosea 4, Obadiah, Matthew 6.21, I Peter 2.11, II Peter 2.19, James 2.13, 4.

Fruit and Leaves

Did you ever see big fruit on a little bush? What's with
that? Huge beautiful stalks of flowers on a plant that
has only a few leaves. How does that happen? Not
everybody has a lot of leaves. Some are severely
pruned. Others just grow the way their told. So
when you see someone with a huge ministry
serving God: big fruit. Then, ask yourself.
Consider. Are you willing?
There's a big
difference
between
desire, determination, and obedience.
Two out
of three
doesn't make you a winner.
And, not everybody is supposed to
have big fruit. Many plants serve us by
their leaves. Have you ever heard of a tea
fruit? How about an aloe Vera fruit suave?
No, there are herb teas for healing and
aloe Vera suave for wounds.
God has different
plants for
different
uses
in the body.
So, consider, maybe
you are meant to be
used with the leaves.
The leaves are for the
healing of the nations. Hey,
I think I would like to be leafy.

Empowers His Word

He knows that you can find what you think you need,
but He wants to provide.
He wants to continue to give to meet your needs.
If God empowers His words, then He didn't stop today.

Afloat

Afloat, adrift, undaunted,
because we don't need to know
where we are going.
Our needs are already met
by the promises He has left.
We just call on them.

Healing of the Nations

Where's the rice paddies?
Flood the foreign field.
Pick up what He plants. Invite the family.
Its the season to work together
for the healing of the nations.
Foreign to foreigners.
We give them God's message from Heaven.
We don't have to understand them. He does.

Receiving from the Hand of God

Generosity flows from a heart that gives.
Give and it will be given to you, shaken together,
pressed down, and poured out. For, the measure that you
give will be given to you and overflowing. The difference
is that we give to people, yet we receive from God.
There is a big difference in receiving from the
hand of people, or from the hand of God.
God's hand
lets go when it is outstretched.
He never takes back what
He has given, unless
we ask. He gives,
yet we don't receive.
What is that about?
Would we ask for salvation,
then when He extends His hand, we refuse?
Would we ask for eternal life, then when we get to
those pearly gates say, "No thanks." I don't think so.
Then, why do we ask for healing, but refuse it when
it comes? It is that we don't recognize its face?
We are sick and pray for healing. He comes
to heal our whole family instead of
one person. Perhaps, we don't
recognize this face of
healing because
our expectation
is too small.
Our desire
under
estimated
our true need.
God help us to pray into our
needs, then say, 'Thank You.'
When You answer us in grand fashion.

Two Seeds

I need two seeds to grow.
There is one seed of the
vision that I have planted in my heart.
The other is the Word of God.
My vision with His provision gives His
face two eyes that the world can see
His ministry through our hands, to them.

Lost Sheep

We praise you, Father, for all you have done.
We praise you, Father, Holy Spirit and Son.
Help us to serve You.
Remind us, Father, that when You came to us,
we were lost sheep in need of a Shepherd.
We still are.

Store Fronts

Why do we put storefronts on buildings? We want to project
an image of bigness; importance, to the community to help
sell our products. We entice them to buy what we offer.
We don't care if they need it, for, we just want to sell it.
We aren't interested in a relationship, we merely want
to
make a living for
ourselves. We put storefronts on
ourselves as well. We project an image to others, afraid
that the one behind it will not be adequate to
sell us to them. We have sold
ourselves short in
the
process. We hide behind what we think we need to
become, rather than being honest with us both.
What would our town look like if we took
off all those fronts? What is inside
each place, would look
the same. So, who
are we fooling?
Not others,
and not
ourselves.
We are
stalling
from
becoming
what we need
to be. Perhaps we
just need a face lift. Jesus
provides the lift to our chin, the
smile to our eyes, the shine to our
face, and the bounce to our step. And, He
is happy to come in the open door of our heart, He
doesn't care about storefronts. They just get in the way.

Our Uniform

God has a unique job for us within His Kingdom.
He has already made our garment. It is laid out
for us in the secret chambers of His sanctuary.
We need to go to His bedroom and put it on.
It is an individual piece of clothing preordained
by the master designer that will fit us
exactly. It is a uniform that
has a pocket to hold
the key to the
K I N G D O M
Of God.
Now find
the key.

Hungry

Hungry?
Come to the
table of the King.
He will provide for you.
He has food from a King to a daughter.
It is all that He wants to provide for His Church.

Gift is like a Bank

Dream:

Your gift is like a bank. It is a picture that keeps giving riches. It is like a video message on television. There are advertisements in the frame. It is like a ticker-tape message with a continually moving message.

Interpretation:

What does a bank do? Holds people's money; riches until such a time as they need it. Then they come and make a withdrawal. It contains what people need. They draw from the gift like a bank. The bank is like the building that holds the money. It isn't the money and doesn't have any control over how much people draw out. Some may draw thousands, others only a few dollars at a time. They come to the bank and learn the status of their accounts. The riches of God are released through our gifts. It is an avenue for God to flow through to others.

The gift is like a picture that keeps giving riches. It sounds like an ATM to me. When we come to one another, we can draw from the vision that God has put into our hearts. Each one of us has been given a special vision. As we continue to develop that vision, God will continue to give us a greater vision. We are to share this with anyone He sends to us. It is a 'free' ATM. The use of the Spiritual Gifts within the Church is like an eternal ATM.

It is like a zap of God's word that is placed into our hearts that can be visualized and recalled at any time. Abstract things become understood because we can picture what God wants to do. We 'develop' the pictures in our darkroom. When we spend time with God alone, He will reveal to us that vision and the training that He wants for us. A picture is worth a thousand words; God wants to work in pictures. It helps people to understand Him best.

What is in the advertisements? An advertisement is a message about something that someone is trying to sell. What are we trying to sell? Whatever God has laid on our hearts is what will be displayed. My message is about intimacy with God. It plays ticker tapes of how He is continuing to speak into our hearts today.

No matter which channel you put my television on, you will get the same message because this is the one He has placed in my heart to share with others.

The messages are displayed in our frames. We are a moving advertisement. We become a moving advertisement on the heart of God. And, how we draw from the ATM for ourselves is shown to others. They see and take notes from our lives.

God has entrusted us with gifts. He is like the king who will return to see how we have used our gifts while He was gone. We are to be good stewards and invest the gifts. It is like putting money into the bank when we do what we are supposed to do with what He gives us. After a while, we will have so much profit that we will overflow to make a return for others as well. Our plate will overflow with more than enough for ourselves and others.

God gives us the seed and the tools to grow the field. He places us in a field and provides the seed and the tools. It is up to us to plant the seed, learn the Word of God, and seek Him for enlightenment through the Holy Spirit as the crop grows. He will tell us when to harvest the crop. He will show us what to do, but we must listen to His voice. He doesn't give us crops, but seed and tools. We provide the ground; the willingness to do His will. We can bank on His bank because it is filled with riches that will never end.

Psalms 13, 119, Proverbs 8, 22, 24, Isaiah 45.3, Luke 19.23, Romans 11, II Corinthians 9, Ephesians 1.7, 3, Colossians 2.2.

She is a Teenager

The Church is a teenager who is nearing
her time of maturity. She is closing in
on the period when she will
marry the Lamb.
The enemy would like to sneak
in and despoil her before her
time ends, when she goes
from betrothed
to
becoming
married.
But,
God
is a faithful Father.
He
is a jealous
God
and One who
will continue to be
there for His daughter
until
such a time as He hands her
off in final marriage to Jesus, Himself.

The Marriage of the Lamb

What an amazing idea. Purity becomes unified
with the Church, God's people. There is a
unification of mind, soul, and body.
He doesn't consume us and take
us over, just pledge to have and
hold forever. It is a fulfillment
of a pledge. It is a ceremony where
our heart becomes intertwined with
His without anything coming between
us. Nothing more is able to come
between
our oneness with Him. The enemy has been
completely put away and no longer comes
between. Our own flesh is not there
and our will
is submitted in a
mutual love relationship
with Him. And, We love as
He loves us. A spiritual unification.

Arise and Look, Church

Arise and look, Church, for the enemy breathes down
your neck. And He will devour any who does not see
him coming. But, I have given you the eyes to
see.
Look through the glasses that I provide.
See through Me. I will provide the
avenue to protect My Church
from the evil one
in
the last days.

Inspire God

The Holy Spirit
is alive to breath
into the Church of God.
Internal, eternal lifeline of healing.
The lifeline inspired through our breath.

Opening the Gifts

The dream:
We have all received boxes on our doorstep. We must bring them into our house and open them up. Then we need to take out of the box, the tools that were given and put them into our cupboard.

Interpretation:
Many of us are being held as slaves, caught in bondage of someone we do not know how to fight. We are just like the Children of Israel who were caught in slavery in Egypt at the time of Moses. We have stacks of bills and little income. We have sick families that are rent with divorce and illness. Our kids are on drugs, and our parents are held in bondages of alcohol, gambling, depression, and suffering. There are bondages that the Devil holds us in. Anything that holds us, making us unable to escape, is bondage. How many times I have talked to individuals and asked them if they feel like they are trying to make bricks without straw? That is what the Children of Israel were forced to do. They were forced to labor for the Pharaoh, then oppressed, and beaten when they could not make enough bricks in a certain time period.

They were not given enough supplies, then whipped when they could not meet the requirements. The Devil puts us there today, as well. Some of us never have enough time, money, and resources to do what we are asked to do. That is the same spirit of bondage that was over the Children of Israel.

The Lord has made a provision for us, just as He did for them. Our rescue comes the same way as theirs did. We need the miracles of God to part the water and help us to move into the Promise Land. We need His help to move into the promises that He has for us.

The freedom of God's people is brought about through us. We are the hands of God that He wants to use to break the bonds for others. God shows His love to others through us. He is showing us His plans, and we are the ones that help to make them work. He is building a spiritual Kingdom that is running a parallel timeline next to the worldly Kingdom.

A problem is that most of the time, we are not aware of the spirit world. But, when we are born again, we are given eyes to see the things of God. His Kingdom can only be seen with our spiritual eyes, the eyes of faith. God wants to share His heart with us; to become intertwined in our lives.

God has left us presents on each of our doorsteps. These are like scrolls that need to be unrolled. They are tied with a string, which is His covenant of love to us. The gift boxes contain the plans for the building of His Kingdom while we are here on earth. Enclosed are insights into His heart. They are like boxes delivered on our doorstep. The Holy Spirit is the Ups Man bringing us whatever is on God's list.

We open the door and bring the package into our house. Then, we lay the package on the table, untie that which binds it and open it. Inside are all the riches of God that He wants to give to us.

We open the door of our heart to receive whatever God has placed on our welcome mat. Our hand turns the key to unlock that door that leads from our own personal 'kingdom' to allow His 'Kingdom' to enter into our house. God doesn't send His children a bad package. He will not give us bad presents because He loves us.

We first need to recognize that we have received a package. We need to look out the window, waiting for the delivery. We should scan the horizon, look for God at work, and for His Kingdom to come. Then, we need to figure out what it means to be part of this spiritual Kingdom. This is through reading the Bible.

The next step is to allow our minds to be transformed to be like Christ. We allow Him to help us to become what He has intended us to be. We walk into the anointing that He has predestined us to. That brings the presence of the Holy Spirit into our house. We have picked up our box and brought it into our house.

The box needs to be set on the table in the kitchen. We must place all of the teachings we receive on the table. We bring it to Him and ask Him about it.

He needs to be the one who cooks up what we learn. The box has a ribbon on it. We need to untie the ribbon: Remove the bow. We enter into a covenant relationship with God. It is one of mutual commitment and love. We become willing to be one of His plants, and He becomes our husband. He is not merely a father but an intimate friend.

After we have opened the box, we remove the gift and put it into our cupboard. There is a combining of the presence of God with the covenants and promises that we have made to one another.

The Seven Spirits of God

There is a progression through the Seven Spirits of God revealed in Isaiah 11. Allow me to walk you through. When we recognize that God loves us, and we start to love Him back, then we have entered into the Fear of the Lord. We learn that He loves us more than we could ever love Him, and it is a bit scary. And, then, we realize that we can never match His love, yet, we continue to press toward Him. That is the fear of the Lord which is the beginning of Wisdom.

When we have fallen in love with Him, then we want to learn all about Him. He has left us a book, the Bible, which tells us a lot about Him. As we begin to read it, we will grow in knowledge. That is the Spirit of Knowledge.

We invite the Holy Spirit to take up residence within us, and He will give us Counsel and Understanding to comprehend the Bible according to the ideas of the writer, God.

We pick up the idea of a commitment with God at this time. He starts to tell us His mind and we are telling Him ours. There communion. With that interaction, He will say to us His ideas of how He wants us to behave and move toward Him. We exercise discipline and obedience to His word.

That is our side of the deal. As our relationship becomes closer, we will feel His presence more and more. This is the Spirit of Presence. He wants to be with us because we are His friend. We want to be with Him because we like Him, too.

Our relationship has grown to the point where we have learned how to listen to His voice within our heart.

He has given us tools, and our hands know how to use them. We not only have the recipe on how to bake the cake, we know how to do it, and He stays with us while we do it. So we start to cook up

His stuff. That is moving into the gifts of the Holy Spirit through the Seven Spirits of God.

For, then, we have progressed to the Spirit of Might, which works miracles because they are acts prompted by God, empowered by Him and flowing from His hand through ours. {*Miracules'* is a book with more information on the Seven Spirits of God. If there is a desire to know more about these Seven Spirits, look for that book. It follows this book.}

Connection between the Holy Spirit, Tools, and Fruits

The tools to open the boxes are wisdom, knowledge, prophecy, and tongues. They are the provision of God for us that gives the faith to believe God for the miracle of His intervention into our lives; His healing.

Wisdom is learning how to view the box from God's perspective. We acquire His mind on things. Knowledge is knowing the sender of the Box. We come to know His gifts by knowing the sender. Prophecy is learning to hear and see God. Opening our spiritual eyes and ears to Him. The eyes of our hearts become open to the eyes of His heart when we move into the prophetic. We see things and hear things. Dreams, visions, voices. Tongues is a language that God gives His children to share Himself with them. When tongues is combined with open ears, there will be an interpretation of tongues. When it is combined with open eyes, there will be visions of the tongues.

We must open the box that God gives us on our doorstep before we can be used with direction in another's life.

We have to get the box open, unwrap it, and put it in our cupboard. If God has sent us a mixer, we need to use it to bake cakes before we can give cakes to others. We can't give the mixer to others. That is not what God intends us to do.

But, we are to take what we find in that box back to Him; to His presence at His table and ask Him what to do with it. Maybe He wants us to make cookies instead of cakes. He will give us tools that can be used for many purposes.

As often as we desire to open the front door of our hearts, God will give us new packages at any time.

The box has to be opened before the presents can be taken out of it. The presents represent all of the riches of God that He desires to give to the Church. They are the fruits of the spirit: His face manifested to us. He puts it in whatever packaging that He wants. His peace may be given to a grieving family. The person who knows how to open a box would open their door to receive what God has for this family. He would pray to God and ask for direction. (Open the Door.) God, then, might give him a vision of a lily. (Word of Knowledge). Then, through the word of wisdom, He takes it to the scriptures. He knows that a lily is a symbol of new life; purity in Christ. So, with this direction, He prays with the family for new life and purity. The prayer has been directed by God through the use of the tools that He has provided.

The fruit basket is the gifts of teaching, prayer, evangelism, preaching, exhortation, mercy, giving, serving, prophecy. This is the package that the gift from God is sent out to His people. {See the books *Festevia'* and *Camezia Reptidad* for information on the gifts of the Holy Spirit. Glorybound Publishing.}

Romans 12.6, I Corinthians 12.8

Just Believing

Just believing is too hard for many. We need to be
careful not to judge others. They need to believe in Christ alone
and Him crucified, but it is not easy. They would do things
differently if they believed.

Adoption Allowance

He brings us to where He wants us to go. He provides
the current for the river. It's currency for now. He gives
us what we need to pay for what we need. His provision.
We come to Him as His children and hold out our hands.
It's our allowance. It's what allows us to do what He asks.
We come asking our Father for the provision that He has
already promised ahead of time. Of course, He will give it.
A covenant was made in advance. We were born again into
a relationship as His child He claimed and adopted us. And,
now, He supports us.
Simple.

Sleeping Church

Sleeping Church, where have all the children gone? The
enemy has snuck in and stolen them while we have slept.
Awake, Church, and gird your loins. Awake, Church.
There is no fight. You only have to see. For when
our eyes are open to the tactics of the enemy,
he is exposed. The minute he becomes
known, he is dismantled and
unable to use his tactics
any longer. Your
Heavenly
Father
will fight him
for you when you call
on Him.
His
power is
adequate against Satan.
Remember, that the Lord created him.
So He knows his ways and can surely unravel
any mystery that he puts together to try to baffle
us. He cannot build a mystery God cannot undo.

Special Project

If you want a special project, you must stay
after school. The teacher has them set
aside for students who have shown
an aptitude and a desire to press
above and beyond, to pursue
excellence.
God's school of Higher
Learning is now
in session
and
He
is
canning
the
horizon
for such students.
Credit
It's OK to do something
and give the credit to someone
else. We don't need credit when
everything we have is paid for, already.

Important Jobs

here is a tendency for us
To
consider some jobs more
important than others.
We base our system
of measuring the
importance on the standards of those
around us. We consider the president to be more
valuable than the aid to him. We see the president,
but
not the aid.
God puts
us
upfront. He puts our face on His actions.
He has become our aid. Yet, I would
not call Him less important,
or His job to be
insignificant.

Calls

The dream:

The telephone is ringing. My brother is there. He looks at the caller ID. It says, "GOD." I know that the phone is for Him, so I tell him to pick up the line. He looks at the caller ID and refuses to pick up the receiver.

Interpretation:

This is an interesting dream. I know that the brother refers to our brothers and sisters in Christ. Sometimes, we see their call, yet they refuse to pick it up. We see their opportunity to serve God come and Go. The question I asked God on this dream was, "Why wouldn't he pick up the phone?"

So, I thought about it for a while. One of the reasons that I don't pick up the telephone when I see the Caller Identification is that I don't want to speak to the individual that is calling. But why would someone not want to talk to God? Perhaps, he doesn't want to hear what God has to say. He is afraid of God's call. I become angry over his refusal to accept God's call. Is that my right? No.

We each have our own relationship with God. How God calls, someone else is none of my business. Maybe, I think that I can clearly see that God is calling my brother, but he is refusing to answer it. My responsibility is to pray for him and encourage him, not become angry with him.

And, what about my brother in the dream? The message of the dream is that we each much individually accept God's call. I cannot receive your messages, and you can't receive mine. We each have our own private line to Him.

Within the dream, my brother refuses to answer the call from God, even though he realizes it is Him. It seems like he is angry at God for not responding to him earlier. Mary felt the same way when she called Jesus to come and heal Lazarus. Jesus waited three days before going there. By the time he got there, Lazarus had been dead for three days.

Mary was mad and told Him that He was late. Jesus' response was that He knew what He was doing. His timing was perfect regardless of what she thought. In the course of His ministry, He had this all planned in so that He could display His power over death. If Lazarus hadn't died, then He would not have been able to demonstrate His power and the relationship He had with His Father.

Sometimes, God is late on purpose. Perhaps we are not ready for the answer, just yet. Perhaps we need to grow in our faith by learning to trust Him for an answer that we do not have in our hand yet. Maybe, He wants to bring the answer in a different way. Perhaps we have asked Him to speak to us through the Scriptures, but He chooses to speak through another individual or a dream. Do we take offense at the timing or the way God responds to us?

Jeremiah 33.3, John 11..

Here are some more telephone lines:

Follow the directory
with respect to the steps.

The Kingdom of God has a directory is like a phone book. It provides us with information on how to keep in communication with Him on a daily basis. He will direct our steps, if we tap into His wire system of communication.

You can't pick up the call
without knowing what it is.

It is like saying, "I'll be happy to do something, but what?" God has provided phone lines to us, the directory, but we need to pick up the receiver to accept His call. He has paid for the call.

Skill Saw

Sometimes I take a saw to the forest. The old growth needs
to come down. It is providing too much shade making My
love seem barren to the new believers in that place.
There is a change in leadership. Out with the old;
In with the new. They had gotten stiff. Dead
wood in My Kingdom. So, I take them
down and float them in the river for a
while. I call them back to their
purpose. Refresh them.
It's a skill saw
A blade used
to saw
with
skill.
When you see what I want
you
to see
and use
the skill I
give you with
My blade, My
Word
you become that saw.
Be plugged into the current.
Prayer changes the Kingdom in the
direction of God's heart. So, when we see
what He desires, and pray in accordance to His
Word, using the gifts He has given us, we are behind
a powerful movement of changing the forest. Refreshing.

Lemon Delight

The plans of God have seeds in them that build other things.
They are like the miracle of the feeding of the five
thousand. The bread keeps multiplying as long as
they continued to break it. When He provides
a vision, and we keep coming back to
Him to develop it, He will multiply it
much larger than we had ever dreamed of.
It is like He gives a pie to us. It can be sliced
into unlimited pieces because each piece has seeds
that would grow another one. The seeds for ministry
are for us as well. When we step into what He wants,
we will be the one who is the most ministered to. We
will be blessed as He leads us through areas of our lives
where we have been broken and defeated in the past to
overcome; be victorious, living within His grace.
His grace will be on display within the ministry.
He will show His love to us. The very things
that have brought the deepest hurts
are the areas that He will bring
the most healing. It will
fill up and overflow to
others within the
boundaries
of His
plan
for
healing in their lives.
Mincemeat pie
Will be
turned
into
lemon delight. When we have
become healed and made victorious, then we
will be ready to serve others. We envision victory,
then live it, to be convincing to others that it is for them.

Walk on Water

There will be a steady talking with the Holy Spirit
when you see the vision and need to walk in it.
Pick up our feet. Walk. It's a beach party.
A shore ministry when you start to walk,
you are on the shore and Jesus is on
the sea. Then, when you continue
to walk, you will be on the same
level on the sea. To get to the
boat, you walk on the
sea.
That is like
walking on water,
just like Peter.
It's the
Same
miracle.
We see
Jesus, He
calls out to us,
and we follow His
voice toward His power. It's a
miracle, But, don't forget, He always
empowers His voice standing alone in a tempest.

Mobile Cleansing Team

Dream:

I went to the center of a foreign country (like Mexico) to help. Those in charge were killing, and we were part of the plan to stop the massacre of the children. I end up on a mobile bathroom/ shower car. It was like a big camper. At first, I think that I am alone, but I learn that there are a lot of people hiding there in the unit.

Later, when I was home, in my own country, I ran into a father. He was looking for his children, and I said they were probably on the mobile cleansing unit..

Interpretation:

God wants to take us to the center of what is foreign to us. He has a Kingdom that is not in this world. It is foreign, but not soil. It is a spiritual Kingdom. Within that spiritual arena, He is going to raise up individuals who will help to bring about the cleansing of the Church. It is like the purification ceremony that a bride goes through before marriage.

The Church is to marry Jesus in the end, but it must be pure to be able to be ready for the wedding. Purity is achieved through cleansing. All of us need to be hiding in the mobile shower car. God has provided a mobile cleansing unit through Jesus' sacrifice for us. At any time, we can seek His cleansing for our sins and become purified.

In the dream, I thought that I was alone. But, the message of the dream is that we are not alone. There are others who need to be cleansed. In fact, there are so many that need cleansing that God is going to sweep through the country and clean up the whole place.

Pre Paired Union

God has already prepared His plans for the union with the hands of those who have a heart with a desire to bring praise to His name. The bride is at her altar and the groom is at the door.

Days of Elijah.

The days of Elijah are here. I will raise Up for Myself prophets who will listen to My heart and share it with others so that all will know who I Am. No more playing Church.

Knowledge of Me

The earth is alive with the knowledge of Me. I share Myself
over and over. Although it is fallen and cursed, I didn't
abandon it. It's like a piece of china, one of a set
that has a crack in it. It goes with the other planets
and I still am served there,
so I keep My presence there until I get a new
set of china. I need enough plates to serve
all of My children. It's like one of those
plates
that you set another plate onto in a
formal dinner. I am a charger. The
children set their plate on Mine
and then they can be fed.
My plate reserves
their place at
the table.
My
world;
Me
shines
through
those glass
plates as they
are set on the table
of My presence.
Indwells
Christ
indwells, where we dwell. Live the love,
for the love is alive. And, He loves to live within
us. To us, in us, through us. Passing us day after day.

Sending the Holy Spirit

The church is crying out, and God has given to her. It is not what she was asking for because she only would have settled for crumbs. He has given a feast.

The progression of our Purpose

God wants to have an ongoing relationship with us. He does not have a physical body, so we can't have a relationship with Him like we have with other people on the earth. He is different. He has sent us help to understand how to relate to Him. When He sent Jesus, it was a big step in our direction because Jesus Christ is the exact representation of who the Lord is. So, if we study Jesus, then we can come to know God. But, the problem is that Jesus lived 2000 years ago and doesn't walk here on earth anymore. How can we get to know Him?

There is a progression of our relationship with God through Jesus that takes place once we have become a Child of God.

First, we learn what He has done for us, then, we learn what He expects of us. How do we know?

It is all about intimacy. We come closer to God, and He desires to become intimate with us just as He is with Jesus. He invites us into His thoughts as we open ourselves up to Him. The interactive relationship with Him via the Holy Spirit will teach us all things about God. He will tell us about the purpose He has for us: One that He has selected ahead of time.

God has a plan to build His Kingdom, and we are the children within it. He has birthed us with the intentions of a job within this Kingdom.

You can believe it that He is waiting, close at hand, to tell us His purpose for our lives. We have hair a particular color and a body, a specific shape, for a reason. We have educational training and family heritage for reasons only known to Him. He does not want to keep it a secret. No. He wants to tell us, then help us walk into that purpose.

I would never have dreamt that I would be writing books, but I remember, now, that several years ago, I was the editor in the High School newspaper. I am sure this helped to prepare me for my future.

He starts by embedding the vision within our hearts. We have been 'stamped' with His seal. He has 'stamped' each of us with a vision for the purpose that we are intended for.

When we learn this purpose, then we can start toward the vision. It will fit like a glove. You know when you find a job that feels right? It is something you never thought you would do, but when it has the stamp of God, it will succeed.

After we learn the vision, then we can move into His training of us. He wants to train us, Himself. How? The Holy Spirit is the manifestation of God's Spirit to us here on earth. He will teach us all about God because He is God. Who best to teach us about some-one but themselves?

God separated Himself into three entities, three manifestations when He sent Jesus to the earth.

At first, God was all together, just like we think we are. But, when He sent Jesus, He broke off the physical manifestation of who He is, from the spiritual manifestation.

God is in heaven, and He is Spirit. Jesus is the manifestation of God that is flesh and came to the earth. The Holy Spirit is the Spiri-tual manifestation of God that was sent when Jesus rose from the dead who indwells us when we ask Him to. In the future, God will join Himself all together again as He joins us to Himself.

The Seven Spirits of God are all are manifestations of God. Prov-erbs talks all about how Wisdom wants to become our trainer.

Wisdom is likened to 'our mother' in the way He trains us. It doesn't mean that God or the Holy Spirit is a woman, but rather, that Wisdom trains us tenderly, with a parental relationship. It is a nurturing type of interaction that we have when we are trained by 'mother' Wisdom.

How do we become trained by the Spirit of Wisdom from the Holy Spirit? God's Holy Spirit talks to our spirit.

The difficulty is that many of us do not know how this works. The Holy Spirit talking to our spirit is like a foreign language, and we do not understand it. If a voice comes to us and we do not understand it, then we cannot follow the commands?

We need to learn how to interpret the messages from God to be able to understand them and be trained into the vision that He has placed in our hearts. It gives insight into the interactive relationship that Jesus was talking about in John when He said, "Abide in me and I in you, because the branch cannot bear fruit unless it abides in the vine."

It is about abiding and learning to listen to the quiet voice of our Lord. Only when we hear that voice, can we have a chance to obey it. He wants us to understand. What a relief to know He is on our side!

Dawn of Awakening

O Wings of the morning, come to us.
Dawn of awakening,
awaken our souls to new life in Thee.
For we long to fly into Your sunrise.
Rise in our hearts, I pray.
I know it's late and we've slept in.
We come like a laborer to be paid early
when we came late.
We call upon Your mercy.
That's all we can do.
That will be enough.
Your wings of mercy carry all.

Pitter, Patter

A love beat plays a song of my heart, Love of my life. Pitter, patter, like feet walking down the hall, I sense Him coming; coming to my door to see if it is open that He may enter. The Holy Spirit is exciting. He comes. Be quiet. Wait. Wait on Him, and He will come. Wait with reverence.

The Dove

Is the Holy Spirit a Bird? No. He just has a lot of
characteristics like one. He doesn't walk, but He
gets from place to place. He does not eat worms,
but He does savor time we spend with Him. He
likes it when we meet. So, I guess you could say
He likes to meet. He does not build a nest or live in a
tree or a cliff. But He does flow from the tree of life;
Jesus Christ. There are seasons
that He follows for specific movements and eras. And, He
does feed His young like a momma bird. He takes what He
takes in, the words from God, and regurgitates them to us
in a form we can swallow. And, He keeps coming back to
'our nest'. He does not sit on us like a bird sits on eggs
until they are hatched. But, He does stand near to
help us when we need it. He is not a dove, but
like a dove. He carries messages from
the Father to us and back. He is a
faithful messenger. It is His
message, as well. Him, the
Father and Jesus are one.
And, He is every
color of the
rainbow.
He is pure and white, the maker of all covenants true.
He is not bound by anything here on earth.
He flies. He is
the wings
of our relationship
with God. He is the one who
enables us to intertwine the Him, spirit
to Spirit, on a different level other than the physical.
He enables the plane of that high relationship. A Window.
There is a window in this house that has not been opened for
years. In fact they forgot it opens. They have painted it shut.
It's a window to heaven. A window of our heart to the Lord's.

Kisses of Wisdom

Our Jesus has left us the Holy Spirit. She is personified in
Proverbs as our mother. She makes us dinner. She serves
us with the words of Jesus to feed our soul. She wants
to be with us always. As our mother, she cries for
us to stay with her. It is not a cry of agony, but
one of a tender mother who is separating from
her beloved child. Her heart is tender for us. We
bring her encouragement each time we respond
to her with thankfulness of her words of hope to
our heart. For we now have hope because Jesus
gave her to us. We are different. We are no longer like
those without hope. And, no matter what happens, we
can always be with our mother, the Spirit of Wisdom that
Jesus has given us. Then, she will kiss us. When we pray
with hope and intimacy, she will kiss us with her presence.
Mother Wisdom prepares the supper for us. She wants
us to join her in the kitchen. It is not the meal, but
the relationship that is built while we cook
together that is what is important. Mother
is making supper. I go to leave and she
cries. Mother is touched and doesn't
want me to go. I hug her and say,
"Remember how it used to be
before I was saved. I had
no hope. Now I have
hope. No matter
What happens,
we can
always
be
together."
Then, she kisses me.
Of course, I will stay for
supper. I would never think of
walking out while she is preparing supper.

No Worry

We can walk into the plan that God has for us without worry because His plan is bound by His eternal love for us. He has an eternal, unending love for His Children. His plan is as alive as He is. He is the fire within that sparks the flame that sets the Word aglow for all to see. He will provide air, fuel and spark for His fire to burn.

Cotton Tail

The hopping cottontail runs when no one pursues him. He runs from noise. Noise without the intent of harm. He doesn't wait to interpret the sound. He just turns and hops away as fast as his little hoppers will take him. Sometimes God brings His presence different than we expect. Instead of asking Him for interpretation of the noise, we run; we high tail it in the opposite direction of the noise. Then, when we are on the far side of the canyon, we become jealous of those near to His voice. It was our choice to allow fear to drive us from God. Ask Him to put it aside. His love will calm that uneasiness of the bunny in you.

Presence of the Holy Spirit in the Church
Bringing God's children into His presence

God wants us to be aware there are hungry children that He wants to feed. We need to put on the glasses that will provide us with the vision He has for the Kingdom and pick up the passion that God has for those who are hungry. The Children of God can't grow if they are not fed. They don't need to drive our ministry, but they need to learn how to come and sit in His presence. They will follow us if we allow them to. We need to take them along on the trip.

The road to the presence of God is through prayer. We need to be the ones to lead the way up the trail into His presence. Others may see the presence of God differently. God is a God of many names and reveals Himself as He desires. He may show Himself to each of us in a unique way, but the outcome is the same; victory and a changed life.

Jesus Christ paid the price for us to see the presence of God, but we need to put on His robe of righteousness. We must be pure, white as snow because God is Holy and cannot enter an unholy place. He has called us to carry His 'vessels'. We are like the Children of Israel who were in the desert when God called them to make them into a nation. He gave them plans for the Ark of the Covenant and assigned jobs for the tribes. When each assumed their position, then the Ark was carried with the people. The Ark contained the presence of God. So, today, it is a symbol of how His presence is to be carried within the Church. It is held within a covenant covered with a Mercy seat. (See Miracules' for a detailed study on the Ark of the Covenant correlations.)

There were many things needed to be ready to perform sacrifices and worship in a mobile fashion. The Ark of the Covenant was so much more than a box that was carried on two poles as they traveled from place to place.

They burned sacrifices with specific directions. And, the sacrifices were not little pigeons and small game. They were everything from oxen to full-grown sheep. Imagine what it would take to slaughter an ox and lay it on an altar to sacrifice. The curtains that lined the walls were 150 feet long on one side. There were many things that needed to be carried along with the table where the bread of presence was placed.

We each carry an aspect of what it takes to put together all the things that bring in the presence of God into a congregation. Just like the Children of Israel in the desert, if we do not do our part with a pure heart, then the whole picture does not come together. If the one who carries the lampstand to light the area that shines the way for direction, is not paying attention to his job, then how will we know to find the Holy of Holies? If someone fails to carry their tools, all will lack because it is a complete place of worship when everyone participates in doing their part.

Another aspect of those who were privileged to carry the Ark of the Covenant is that of purification. We need to purify our lives from sin. We cannot expect God to bring us His presence when we continue to harbor sin. As they had cleansing ceremonies, we need to follow the same example. Not that we need to have ceremonies, but, we need to get into a habit of daily cleansing our hearts and lives, and asking God to purify us.

The Lord is purifying the Church to make Her ready to be presented to Jesus Christ as a bride without spot or wrinkle. It is a symbolic marriage that will take place in the end times. The Church will become united in body with Jesus. We will give up our own body to His purposes. But, we need to be like a virgin bride when we come. We have been unfaithful, but He will restore us to the same purity that we have had before. It is just like a young virgin who has been unfaithful, God is asking to take us back. He wants us to return our intended purpose. We have been a working wife, but He wants us to become a stay-at-home-one. Purity is provided through the blood of Jesus Christ, but we must ask for it.

He will go before us and come after us. He will pad the way. The Lord brings His presence to us like rain. It sprinkles down from heaven. People will see things that they have not been told and understand things that they have not heard. He will pour out sight, open eyes that are spiritually blind, and give an understanding of Himself directly into their hearts. This is the latter rain of God.

For He is coming down from heaven to relieve our dry hearts and rescue us.

A problem that we have is that we try to interject our ideas into the instructions from the Lord. These ideas look good, just like beautiful flowers, but they don't last past the season.

In fact, if a wind comes along, all of the beautiful flowers will fall down flat and die. Our words apart from the eternal Word of God will fall flat and die in time. We need to have an eternal ministry, not a temporary one

When we build our own ministry, God doesn't like it. He wants to direct us with His eye upon us. He wants to personally feed His little lambs with a special diet. He has prepared fried chicken for us to eat at the coffee table. It is meat covered with His bread, cooked up with the Holy Spirit and boxed, delivered to our door. We eat the meat delivered to us on the table of His presence. For, that is where He is. If He orders the chicken, then He wants to eat it with us. Remember, we are the kids, and He is the dad. He wants to share in the relationship.

Exodus 26, Psalms 3.3, 28.2, 63.4, 91.12, 121.1, 123.1, 134.2, 143.8, Isaiah 40, 52.13, 53.12. Luke 7.35, Thes. 3.12

Ablaze

Awesome God of love, come into my heart today.
Set my soul ablaze.
Ignite the passion within me that You have not yet shown.
Become anew in me.

Your Holiness

Your Holiness exceeds our expectation
of who You are, O God!
Why should we be surprised when Your Holy Spirit
lives within us and makes us become
more than we have ever thought possible.
O to dream His dream!
Be His vision!
Be His feet, His hands, His mouth!
To walk His walk, talk His talk,
to act like the very Savior Himself!
What an awesome concept made possible
through the Holy Spirit living inside us!

Sandwiched
Between
Sleep and Awake

When God turns the light on, we begin to see
things His way. We go from sleep to awake.
There is a certain level that the noise
reaches when we wake up. We hear. We
don't see first, we hear, then, we see.
We are sandwiched
between
now and later, and listen.
Learn to listen. Get yourself a ride
to, between now and later, here
and eternity; the place where
His voice meets His
power. The lighted
place where
we
see
things
as
He does.
Over, under, around,
and thru. Where's thou?
Down the middle. The cleft.

Spirit Hum

Wondrous thoughts from Him to us. From a King
to a daughter. O that we may lounge, bask, and
delight in Your company. Spirit to spirit communion.
Welcome to God's world!
The place where dreams are what is real. He speaks truth
into our spirit. It's a coordinated effort, you know. You
can't just split a personality down the middle and say
God runs one hand while we use the other. He's not
like a puppeteer, either, where we present a frame,
an empty body, and He fills it with His hand.
He doesn't pull us like a donkey laden with
goods is pulled along a trail. He pushes
us like a magnet. We push Him and He
pushes back with a little more force than
we used. That's the Fear of the Lord in action.
The two magnets come together and they don't
stick, but repel. They push because they are alike.
He puts us on a track like a train. Then, we turn to
notice He's on the same track ahead and behind.
We fire up our magnet, our love relationship
toward Him. Then, He sandwiches us between
Himself and pushes us with the current that
flows through the air like two magnets.
When we are on track, aligned
with the Scriptures
and listening
to the
voice
of the
Holy Spirit,
then, He can move the train as
fast as we are willing to push. It's our push
that ignites the air current that He stands behind

Experience the Power

My experience with Him.

On Saturday night at a women's retreat, the pastor came and spoke to us. Then, he prayed over anyone who desired. Everyone he touched fell down. He would go back to people time after time each time they got up. We were thoroughly 'drunk' in the Spirit. I remember rolling on the floor laughing with my girlfriend until she couldn't get up any longer.

I went down three times, then the pastor came to me, and He said, "Look at the mighty intercessor, She is just getting silly now."

I realized that he was right. I had come looking for the diamond that I had been praying for a month. I had done many Bible studies on the sword of the Word. I was asking God to show me how to fight with His sword. I realized that His sword had a diamond tip. The diamonds are like jewels of revelation that He gives to us that make us smarter than the enemy. When we use what He gives us, then we can defeat all our enemies.

And, at this time in the meeting, I realized that if I wanted something from God, I was going to have to show Him that I was serious. I had fasted for a month before this extended prayer time, anticipating that God would meet me at whatever level I was willing to go with Him. I did not know what to expect, but I knew that God had more to give, and I wanted it. I wanted whatever He had for me behind door number one. I wanted the rest of the blessings. And, I know that they included more presence, more power, and more holiness in my life. So, I got up and started praying to Him. I prayed so hard that I began to get chest pain. I surrendered myself totally to Him begging Him to give me MORE. I continued to press-in to Him.

Then I saw IT coming. I saw the Power of God hovering over me, ready to touch down. It looked like the end of a huge drill bit. It was the most beautiful thing that I have ever seen.

When it came down, it didn't hit my head first, but the very center of my heart. It was beautiful light that swirled and swirled right through the center of my being. The colors were flowing through me. They were turquoise, royal blue, and royal purple. There was a single gold thread woven through all of them. Everything was alive and moving. I was lost in it; totally engulfed in the most wonderful feeling and beautiful priestly colors that I had ever know, or ever will know, I am sure. The swirling light cut through my very core and continued to swirl.

It was a boring light that encircled my entire body and never came out. It was a motion of light and feeling. Somehow the swirling colors picked me up and airlifted onto the rug.

When I regained consciousness, there was an overwhelming desire to praise God. I couldn't get off of the floor for several hours. I just laid there and sang praises to God.

They stepped over me as they packed up the room for the night. I didn't care, I was praising God from the floor. After probably 2 or 3 hours, I'm not sure I went to my room. There, I continued to lay on the floor and praise God. After a while, I moved to the bed. But, I continued to praise God. I turned the music down at 2 a.m. ...then back on at 4 a.m. starting in again.

Presence of God with Gifts: Adorning

God is the king, and He has chosen us as kings here on earth to reign with Him. The goal of a king is to unify his kingdom. God longs to bring unity within the Church at His altar of presence. We become unified as we take our robes of royalty and claim our position within the Kingdom of God. Victory comes in our lives because we have adorned the righteousness of Jesus and taken it into battle with us against the enemy.

We must bring the clothes that we wear to the altar of God. We bring our own righteousness, all of the good deeds that we have done, and give them to God. Then, we receive training from Him as to the job He has for us. When we lift up to God what we have brought, He shows us His glory. When we see His Glory, we praise Him for His loving kindness and goodness. He has taken our rags and transformed them into a royal robe. He has taken our sin and given us a robe of righteousness.

Then, we give Him our hearts. When we give Him our heart and ask Him to give us His heart, He will come inside of our heart and fill it with His Holy Spirit. When the Holy Spirit fills our heart with His fire, He will take away all of our desire to compete with Him for His glory. It becomes no longer our temple, but His, dedicated for His service. When this temple is dedicated for His use, His presence will remain. If we bring in our own idols and set them up next to His throne, the glory will depart. We will be left to run our own lives. If we want to run our own lives, even after we are saved, He will let us. We will reap the consequences. At any time, we can pick up our 'rags' rather than the royal robe that He has laid out for us.

We are like a lamp stand to others. We have the oil of the Holy Spirit flowing into us. Then, we hold in our hands the light. It is the ability to interpret God through the gifts that He has given us. This illumines our path.

The higher we hold the lamp, the higher we hold God up in our lives, the further we will see down our path into the will He has for us within the Kingdom of God.

God is captivated by watching the Holy Spirit flow through us when we train with Him. It is like a parent sending his child to gymnastics, then attending a meet. The parent is captivated by what the student has learned from the trainer He has provided. The Holy Spirit is our trainer who will teach us all things. He will help us to live on earth and display the many faces of God. The more we pay attention to the training, the more agile we will become in the hand of God. When He has special missions for us, we will be ready because we are in good condition for them.

When we adorn ourselves with the Wisdom of God, the covering is made. His wisdom within us makes what we show the world, the face of God to them demonstrated through us. God gives us the material and places the spindle in our hand to weave the directions that He has for us. This directs our lives in the direction He has ordained to bring about His Glory and favor to us.

When we realize how much He loves us, then we want others to know how much He loves them. He will train us on how to show His love to others. But we must learn how to listen to Him. He has a pattern for our life already in His hand. It is like a complex weaving. But He has given us the spindle.

Our mouth prays His kingdom into action, our hands reach out to others, our voice shares the gospel, our heart extends soul to soul with others. He trusts us as princes to wear His robes.

It is like God is assigning us each positions of priesthood to carry parts of the Tabernacle to rebuild the Ark of the Covenant so that His presence can abide among the people. The gifts are the job that God assigns each priest. He gives us a portion of the tabernacle to carry. Only when we assume our position, can we actually become part of the entrance to the Glory and presence of God.

There were panels of curtains, veils with angels on them.

There were ten; two groups of five joined together. God uses our five fingers, just as the five curtains, and adorns them with angels. We become the angels of God, visible to the earth to provide an entrance into His tabernacle here. We are the weavers of the veil. We must weave it according to His instructions, then let Him tear it apart to separate flesh, soul and spirit. There is a standing within the Kingdom of God that must be recognized in order to be able to go through the veil; to open the veil for them to see His mercy, His love, His angelic beings coming to their aid. The angels are on the veil (the screen) because they help with the entrance to His presence.

There is a mixture of cleanness and desperation that brings in His presence and His fire. His fire cleanses out the impurities.

The enemy will mimic God's robe of righteousness. He will help us to cover our idols with purple fabric. The difference is that these idols are not alive. They cannot pass on any life to others. If we have idols within our own temple, we can make them to look like they are of God. We can tell ourselves that this 'mission' is of God, yet perhaps, we have a different agenda. Maybe, we want to be noticed, rather than God. This is an idol of 'self-worship'. Even though we cover it with purple robes, it will not have eternal value within the kingdom of God. We will become discouraged and fail.

Why did the soldiers put a purple robe on Jesus? He had said that

He was King of the Jews. They were looking for a conqueror King that would rescue them from oppression. They did not recognize Him when He showed up as a humble servant. They thought He was mocking the Scriptures because they didn't understand them. It is impossible to interpret God's word without knowing Him. The whole purpose of the Bible is for Him to show us His love.

If we never learn how to love Him, we will not know what the Bible means. Someone can jot a message on a piece of paper. If you know the person intimately, then it will mean the same thing to you as it does to the person who wrote it. But if you do not know the person, then the message will not be interpreted correctly.

Often times, the presence of God shows up, and people don't recognize Him because they don't know Him. The more intimately you know someone, the further off you will recognize Him. You know, not only His voice and His form but His mannerisms. The adornment of God is more than robes. It is Him.

Exodus 26.1, 36.35, 39.1, Numbers 4.13, Judges 8.26, 2 Chronicles 3.14, Esther 8.15, Proverbs 31.22, Song of Solomon 7.5, Jeremiah 10.9, Mark 15.17, John 19.2

Joy and delight

Joy and delight, delight and glee,
in Me with you, and you with Me.

Hum

That's the
Holy Spirit hum, My love.
The hummingbird hums when it flutters its wings.
When your heart flutters for Me, My heart flutters back.
Be My bird. Take flight,
or just buzz around in circles. It's the passion of love
welling up and over into your flesh. The Spirit over
coming the flesh.
Good Idea.

Prayer for Bread

O Glorious and awesome God, descend on us, I pray. Give us Your bread from Heaven to feed our souls. Your presence, Your glory, Your beauty. Magnify Yourself through our lives. Display Your likeness in our faces. May Your face shine through to ours and be what the world sees. Not us, but You. O Magnificent One, be honored, I pray. Amen.

Giraffes

Where are My giraffes, the long necks?
Those willing to stick their necks out for Me?
Lay it on the line?
Hiding in the eucalyptus trees looking for things to soothe
their own souls instead of Mine.
The length of your neck shows the end of your commitment
to Me. How about a stretch of your faith?

Luke Warm

Tepid water won't burn.
But, it won't refresh, either.

Be Tested

Tepid water is for bathing babies.
They are not mature enough to handle extremes well.
Don't be afraid to be tested. For, when you are tested,
then you will be proved.
For, it is then that you will learn to go from crawling,
to walking, to running, the race that is set before you.
Be one, to not be afraid of stepping into water,
that doesn't feel right. Take a step of faith.
Walk in places, anew.

Concur to Incur

Concur with the Holy Spirit, God, and Jesus,
to incur His blessings into your life. Incur
love, power, and forgiveness. Concur
intimacy, unity, and direction.
Live the love, for the love is
alive, to live in, and through
you. Concur with His plan,
because you are the incur.
In and through, your hand,
His Kingdom comes.
It occurs as we concur
And allow Him to incur.
Concur to Incur
When your
incur
becomes
concur, Then I can
convey My
mind.
For,
My
mind comes
through with Me,
then
there will be an occurrence
of convergence. My current in you.

The Gifts of the Holy Spirit

What are Spiritual Gifts?

A gift is something that is given from someone to someone else because He loves him. That's it. God gives us gifts because He loves us. He gives us presents.

There are two kinds of presents He gives. He gives His gifts, and He gives Himself. It is like He is a Father giving His daughter a present on her birthday. He gives the gift and wants to sit nearby to see the look on her face as she opens the package. He has many gifts for us and wants to be there when we open them. He has presence with His presents.

A spiritual gift is supernatural and not of this world. It is like a lightning bolt in that it comes from heaven to earth with a great power and we have no control. It is a touch down of the Kingdom of God on earth. Often, we don't recognize when God touches down. Psalm 18 is my one of my favorite passages of Scripture. Someone is crying out to God because he is drowning. His enemies are winning and he is losing. When he cries out, God tears open the heavens and flies down on the wings of the Dove. He parts the water rescues the one who is drowning and fights his enemies for him.

Spiritual gifts are used this way. When I pray over someone who asks me to, then I ask God for direction. He parts the heavens comes down and rescues us. He gives His words, then, sends the rest. He gives comfort, grace, mercy, love, and all the rest. He fights the enemies for the individual because he has cried out to God. The exciting thing about this type of prayer is that God uses us as a screen between them and Him. He puts the words into our mind, gives us a voice, and helps us to pray the way that is needed. We push through to victory, enabled by His grace with the provision of the gifts.

When I pray, I usually speak in tongues, very slowly, one word at a time. Then, I interpret as I go, for the individual. God's voice comes to their rescue. It is amazing.

Why does He give them?

God touches down to earth because He wants to share His world with us. He wants us to abide in Him and Him in us. That is where the combined presents come in. He wants to come live in us. The Holy Spirit was given to help us understand the Kingdom of God and His ways. He is the abiding presence of God on earth. When we reach out and open our hearts to Him, then we invite Him into us. We go to Him, and He comes to us. Then, our spirit is given life. By the indwelling power of the Holy Spirit, we can walk with God's presence.

The presents of the Holy Spirit makes us able to walk. We are sinners. We stumble and fall, going from one bumble to the next as we try to do what we think God wants us to do. But when we invite the Holy Spirit to help us, He empowers us. He gives us the ability to do the things we dream of.

If you want the abiding of the Holy Spirit pray:

My Lord and Father, please forgive me of my sins. I ask you to cleanse me through the blood and power of the Lord Jesus Christ. I renounce Satan and all his friends. Come into my heart, I pray. I ask, also, that You might give me the Holy Spirit into my heart. I want to be made new, afresh, and to walk alive within Your presence each day... Amen.

With the Holy Spirit, you need to be prayed OVER. What this means is that the Holy Spirit is imparted. It is passed through someone who has Him. The disciples imparted the Holy Spirit with laying on of hands. So, we should do the same today. Find someone who has the Holy Spirit to lay hands on you and pray over you in tongues. Then, you will have a complete package. To receive the gift of tongues, ask. Like this:

Father, can I have the gift of tongues. Then, close your eyes, open your hands, your heart, and your mouth.

For, the gift of tongues comes out of our mouth. The words are given by God, but we are the air behind the breath. It is about be-

ing open to receive what God has to offer and open to allow it to flow through you. It is about releasing your own control and turning it over to Him. You can start by saying parts of words. I have those I pray over, say vowels and sort of copy what I say as I speak in tongues. They can feel the Spirit welling up from within. He comes from the center of their heart and pushes the language up from inside. They get a sense of warmth like hot oil is being poured into them.

If I pray over someone who comes to me asking for the gift of tongues, and he doesn't speak in tongues right then, it is because he has not opened up to receive. It is about learning to be open. We may think that we are open, but God is the one who really decides who is open. Because, when God sends His Spirit, He does not give it by measure.

When He comes, all of Him arrives.

And, He does not give to one who asks and not to another. He gives to all of His children. It's just that if your child comes to you and asks for a cookie, then refuses to open his hand to receive it, there is no way to put it into his hand. We are the same way. If we ask God for the gift of tongues, yet do not have a heart that has been washed of our sins, and is ready to receive from His Holy hand, then we can not expect to.

So, if someone comes to me, and I pray for him to receive the Holy Spirit and the gift of tongues, but he does not feel like he got it, then I assign him to go talk to God in greater detail. He needs re-mediation from the School of the Highest God. There is a block, and usually, it is sin. God will reveal his sin, clear the block, and allow him to receive the blessings that are waiting for him. Fasting is very useful when accompanied with an extended prayer time.

A Tree of Gifts

Spiritual Gifts are easily understood using a tree illustration. Suppose there is a fruit tree. This tree has the fruits of the Spirit on it. Galatians 5.22 lists love, joy, peace, patience, kindness, goodness, faithfulness, gentleness, and self-control. When we come under the tree, we bring our basket. We hold our hands up to the tree, and the fruit falls off into our hands. We gather it into the basket that we have brought.

If we have jars, then we can the fruit and prepare it to be spread on bread later for others. (This could be a song, a poem, or a piece of art.) We each bring a different basket to that tree where the gifts are. We carry those gifts tucked in the basket that God has given us, bringing them to others. In this way, we share God with them using the vehicle that He provides. We all receive the same gifts of the Holy Spirit from the tree of life, but carry them in different modes. We strive to gather all the gifts, yet carry them in our own individual manner.

Charismatic Gifts

The charismatic gifts are the means within the vehicle. They provide the direction, the power, the ability, the motion of the vehicle as it moves.

The primary purpose of all of the presents from God is to help His children. Isaiah 61 is a good list of what God intends to do using the charismatic gifts through His Children.

He came to preach good news to the poor
How we are poor. We are in need of a Savior today.

He wants to bind up the broken hearted.
Our hearts have been repeatedly broken by those who we have entrusted them to. We need some gauze to repair our wounded hearts.

He proclaims freedom to those who are captives.
We need freedom. We have been bound by our sins. We have

depression, lust, agony, sadness, anger, pain. We need freedom. We have illness, bad situations, and we are in jail.

There is release from darkness for the prisoners.
We are in the dark until God shows us who He is. We have no light unless He gives it to us. He needs to lead us to Himself. He will lead us as we seek Him.

He is telling of His redemption for us from our enemies.
God wants to use us to put down the ways of Satan and lift up His Kingdom. Prayer is what exchanges one kingdom for the other. When we call on the vengeance of God, His might will put Satan in his place.

We bring God's comfort all who mourn.
The Holy Spirit is our comforter. He will be our resting place amidst the storms that we face.

God is provision for those who grieve in Zion. He wants us to be aware that we can have a crown of beauty instead of ashes, the oil of gladness instead of mourning, and a garment of praise instead of a spirit of despair. Then we will be called oaks of righteousness, a planting of the Lord for the display of His splendor. ....You will be named ministers of our God.

God wants to provide for us because we are His children. He is holding a crown for us that is just like a King gives His children. The crown is a symbol of our relationship with Him and promise of inheritance. A Kingdom backs the crowns that we hold.

Paw Prints

Paw prints leave impressions
in the sand. You can tell if it's
a dog or a lion from the prints.
Follow the prints: the impression.
The impression always leads to it.
When God leaves impressions,
they always lead to Him.
They are different
impressions
given
from
the
same God.
All
foot
prints
through
the sands of
time to a timeless
being; an eternal presence.
Heart Service
Through the Spirit of Life we have been
given freedom to live in this world serving
God with our heart, not our hands. Heart service.

Our Spirit

We are divided into three parts. We are body, soul and spirit. Our body is what we use to walk with, our soul is our will, and our spirit is the part of us that can understand spiritual things. To understand the things of God, we must look at Him through our spiritual eyes.

How do we see with our spirit?

We must become open and broken. We must allow God to break us apart; to show us the difference between our flesh, spirit, and will. The flesh is that part of us that wants the lemon pie when we are on a diet. It calls to us, "Eat it, and you will be happy."

The soul is that part of us that helps plan our own future. We plan what we want to do and try to do it. We exercise our will when we don't snap back at the rude grocery clerk. Our will drives our flesh to make our mouth not open up and say nasty comments back.

Our spirit is the third part of our being. We commune with God our spirit to His Spirit. We 'feel' Him with our spirit because He is Spirit. We cannot see God because He is not flesh, so He has made a provision for us to be with Him all of the time. He talks to our spirit. Our spirit talks back to Him.

That is how we can pray without moving our mouth. We pray with our spirit. This part of our being is pushed and pulled through our hearts; through love. What we love, moves our spirit. Those who love us move our spirit. You know. You can 'want' to love someone, yet, you cannot. Then, there are those you don't want to love, yet, you do. That is our spirit driving us.

God wants to move us through our spirit. He wants to move our heart to connect it with His. That is the Fear of the Lord. This fear is not something we are afraid of. It is when we realize enough of the love of God that we are drawn back from Him because of the intensity of it.

Judgment and Mercy of God
VS the Fear of God

The Fear of the Lord does not mean that we are afraid of Him. Our Father does not want us to be afraid of Him any more than our natural father does. There is a fear of God because He is the creator of the universe and one that is in control of life and death, yet we should not fear Him. Those who face judgment without having Jesus on their side will fear Him, however, He is not their dad. We only are His children when we have become adopted into the family. To be adopted into the family of God, we must be born again and accept the adoption papers that have been left for us by the Father. Jesus paid the price for our adoption into the spiritual family of the Father. But, on the contrary, if we do not accept the adoption papers, and ask Jesus to forgive our sins while we are on the earth, then we should fear the judgment of the wrath of Him. For, God has made Jesus to be the one who judges us for our sin. The penalty for sin is death. We all will die in our sin because of the wrath of God.

It is not that He is mean, but it is the nature of His personality. The two arms of God are mercy and justice. Justice is the aspect of God that demands payment for sin. It is what will bring about the destruction of Satan. It is the Holy part of God, where He cannot stand in the presence of sin. He would if He could, but He can't. When He is confronted with sin, He loses His temper. He hates sin.

The other arm of God is His mercy. (Not to say that God has only two aspects of His character, but these are simple.) Because He knew that He had a problem with getting angry over our sins, but still wanted to be able to become our Father and have a personal, close relationship with us, He made a provision to fix the problem. It is like He is King Kong, and when each time he would pick up the screaming woman, he would squish her without knowing it. (Of course, that didn't happen because it was a movie.) But, the analogy is real.

If God couldn't stand us because of our sin, then, how would He ever be able to get close to us?

Isaiah 59 says that because there was no one else that could do it, He did it Himself. It was a problem between the holiness of God and the sinfulness of us.

Only God, Himself could bridge the gap to bring about our salvation. So, He devised a plan and sent Jesus. Now, Jesus was holy, yet He was a man living in a sinful world. He died and paid the price for our sinfulness. The price is death. It is the expected payment to God. It is not to Satan. He has no part of the deal. He is just a trouble maker. It is God that demands payment for sin. We cannot barter with His price because He is the one who gives us breath. If we cannot pay the price, we stop breathing; we die.

The hand of mercy that was extended by God, acted through His love for us, worked a plan where He filled in the gap between Himself and us. In essence, God, who was Jesus in the flesh, died on the cross for us, ascended into Hell, and was judged by His own nature. It's kind of like when a son is bad, and he comes to his father. The father knows that he has a temper problem, so rather than hitting his son, he punches the wall breaking his own hand. He loves his son so much that he doesn't want to strike him, but he is overwhelmed by his anger.

God is not angry, but He does have an aspect of judgment within His character that demands holiness. So, what He did was like a father who would be angry at his son. God took our penalty on Himself (His Son, Jesus) even to the point where He 'died'. But, because He couldn't be killed, He rose from the dead and defeated death for all eternity. And, when He conquered death, He also defeated Satan, Sin, and a myriad of other problems that we had. You see, Satan is the accuser. He accuses us before God of our sin. And, he is right when he comes to God because we are sinners. So, when he goes to God with accusations of our sins, he called them to God's attention, prompting the aspect of God's character in the realm of judgment.

Then, Satan has 'legal' papers against us, which enable him to torment our lives because of our sin.

When we come to God daily and ask for forgiveness of our sins, known and unknown, then Satan has no opportunity to accuse us before God. We need to keep our slate clean and keep him out of our lives. The way to keep Satan off our backs is when he comes, and accuses us of sin, to ask God about it. When we ask Him, and He tells us, then we confess it and seek repentance for it. This takes the wind out of the sails of Satan's death vessel. This puts our spirit in constant communion with the Holy Spirit because we become holy as God is holy.

Isaiah 48.9, 59.16

Light Bright

Be My de light. Delight in thee
My Savior to me.
E're He found me, I was lost.
E're I claimed Him as my own.
Delight prescribed, described and subscribed
by Him beforehand. Awesome!

Kitchen Utensil

In God's kitchen there are no
ready-made mixes.
There is not a bunch of appliances.
There is just us.
When He wants to make dinner for the children,
He stirs one of us.
When our heart is stirred, we emit colors that reflect Him.
Hearts moved for Him,
is His only utensil in the kitchen of the house of His Wisdom..

Hearing Clearly

People stop and stare. It does not come their way often. A soul who hears from God clearly enough to copy it down, then, do it, and it works. Miracules'. Love in action. Grace in motion. Like watching a pair of whales dance. Awesome power with graceful direction.

Transparency

The gifts of the Holy Spirit, the 7 Spirits of God are demonstrated through us when we are open to Him. (Fear of the Lord, Wisdom, Understanding, Knowledge, Presence, Counsel, Might outline in another book *Miracules*). These are in Isaiah 11. The Holy Spirit flows to us, then, in us, then it can flow through us, to others. We must learn how to become open. It is about becoming transparent.

For example, the Spirit of Council will tell us what is on the mind of God. But, we have to put aside our own plans for the situation. We must become open to God's ways. We have to turn over ourselves to Him, lay ourselves on the altar, and become a living sacrifice. It is only after we have done this, that He can make His plans alive within our lives. After they have become alive in us, then He can use us for others.

Every gift that is given to others within the Kingdom of God has to flow through our own lives. If we intend to use the gift of mercy to help someone through the pain of a loss, then we have to become willing to feel their pain. The gifts meet in us. The person meets the power of God at us. We are on the wall between the Kingdom of God and them. We become the link between God and others. It is as if we are the hands of God to them.

The safety net that He gives us to make sure we demonstrate His heart is the way the Gifts of the Holy Spirit flow. If we are not willing to open up with God and with others, the gifts do not flow.

We must become open and broken. The openness makes us to be the hands of God and the brokenness provides direction because we know how to listen as He directs us through His Spirit. Then, when, He shows us something in the spirit world, we ask Him for faith to believe it, and grace to walk into it.

Flow of Gifts

A look at nine gifts in I Corinthians Chapter 12

Prophecy is a gift that helps to understand the voice of God.

He comes to us, but we can't hear because we are not sensitive to His voice. When we become sensitive to His voice, then we will hear it. Hearing it is one thing, we need to ask the Holy Spirit to help us interpret it. He is the one that brings it to our conscious mind and gives us the ability to understand it.

Prophecy has to do with the voice of God. When the Bible was canonized, God did not quit speaking. He continues to speak today. He talks in dreams, visions, in an audible voice, into our spirit in a quiet voice, and through hundreds of other ways, we don't even know. He speaks through creation. Once, in the Bible, He spoke through a donkey. God is God and can speak any way He wants. Listen up.

Prophecy to others helps them to hear God's voice. Someone with the gift of prophecy 'unrolls the scroll so that others can run with it.' The person with this gift has become tender to the voice of God and is able to deliver His messages for others. Every prophet is living the verses of Isaiah 61 if he is truly a prophet sent by God.

The gift is demonstrated in as many baskets as people bring to the tree of life. There are artists who paint and artists who sing. They both help us to understand the voice of God. There are book writers, and there are preachers. These are vehicles that God uses to manifest the gift of prophecy. We all need to become prophets of God. For, we all need to hear God's voice and interpret it so we can know what He wants us to do. After we interpret it for ourselves, then we can press toward being used in other's lives.

Knowledge gives insight to who God is.

Again, there are as many vehicles as there are people with it. Again, there are as many vehicles as there are people with it. Anyone who helps us to understand God's character has this gift. The gift of knowledge has the privilege to information that could only be known of by God. Many times individuals with this gift are confused with clairvoyants and palm readers.

Wisdom *relays God's heart regarding a situation.* Sometimes, it is difficult to tell the difference between the gifts because they are all mixed up like a cake. God mixes them up and bakes whatever He wants within the individual. Wisdom tells the mind of God, council tells His plans. For the most part, the gift of Knowledge reveals the diagnosis of a problem, and the gift of Wisdom tells the answer to it. Wisdom is God's heart on a matter. Knowledge gives the details of it, whereas Wisdom tells how to fix it. This gift is easily seen when someone prays over another in tongues, then gives the interpretation. The interpretation is the words from God, so it is disseminated through the gift of Wisdom.

Discernment *has a sensitivity to be able to see the enemy.* Those with this gift can see the goal and know it is as good as done. Those with the gift of faith believe God's word. They must have the gift of prophecy first, because they need to hear the voice of God and interpret it for themselves.

Only, when they interpret the voice, can they see the outcome. They believe that God's word is alive and that His plans are as good as done. They, also, must have nearly all of the other gifts. This one is on the top of the list. It is a rare gift that is closely related to the gift of miracles. To get to the miracles, one must believe God for them.

Faith *is the ability to see the end before it is here.* Those with this gift can see the goal and know it is as good as done. Those with the gift of faith believe God's word. They must have the gift of prophecy first, because they need to hear the voice of God and interpret it for themselves.

Only, when they interpret the voice, can they see the outcome. They believe that God's word is alive and that His plans are as good as done. They, also, must have nearly all of the other gifts. This one is on the top of the list. It is a rare gift that is closely related to the gift of miracles. To get to the miracles, one must believe

God for them.

Miracles is a gift given to one who knows how to get out of the way quickly.
One with the gift of miracles simply believes God and has learned how to become open and broken. He allows the Spirit of Might to flow through. These are supernatural occurrences that happen by the flow of the Holy Spirit. Salvation and deliverance ministries need the gift of miracles.

Healing is a gift that brings mending to others. Those with the gift of healing have learned how to hear the voice of God, pray into it and walk in that direction. God is a healer. This gift is very closely tied to the gift of Mercy. For, one needs to feel with the individual that hurts, to be able to know how to help him pray. It is one who is selfless and able to move out of the way quickly. God does not entrust this gift to those with pride. Only those with humility can be trusted with this gift because they need to be able to move aside quickly to give honor to God.

Tongues is speaking in a voice given from God. It comes to us when we open ourselves up to the Holy Spirit and start to commune with Him Spirit to spirit. His voice wells up within us to bring praise to Him.
Our spirit wants to praise Him, and when we receive the Baptism of the Holy Spirit, it releases our spirit to praise Him.
It is a foreign language. It may be a language that is alive or one that is dead. They are individual. It is His words directly spoken into the spirit of the individual. When the person opens his mouth, the strange language flows out. People provide the air, the mouth, and the motion, while God provides the words.

Interpretation of Tongues is able to tell the group what someone said when he spoke in tongues. The gift of prophecy is the gift of interpretation of the voice of God. The gift of interpretation of tongues is like the second course in the class. The gift of prophecy interprets the voice of God from the person's spirit to make it understood in a language we speak.

This gift goes the other direction. It is like learning to speak Spanish. First, we interpret English to Spanish. Then, when we get better with the language, we can interpret Spanish to English.

Tongues is God's language. It has to go through the mind, then the spirit of the person with the gift, then, be interpreted back around the corner to be understood. To be open to receive this gift, one needs to be open to God, his own heart, and the hearts of others. It involves a three-way open channel. For, the other person speaks his 'tongues' given by God, then they come to the interpreter. Now, he must send them back to God for the interpretation. He is the one that supplies it. Of course, He puts it into his heart, and he must interpret it into his mind through his own spirit. It requires a lot of open channels. Therefore, we don't see it very often, but it is very powerful when it is present. All of the titles to the books are tongues with interpretations because I have this gift.

Exodus 25.31-40, 27.20, Proverbs 6.16, 9.1, Isaiah 11, 30, Jeremiah 23.29, Zechariah 2-4.

Son Light

The Son light is way too bright to look into without
your I covering. When your eye connects with His
eye then you can wear the Holy Spirit: your Son
glasses. Put your heads together. His
headship and your will and put
the ear pieces on.
Hear from Him. Then,
you can look into the Son: See the beauty of
Him. His radiance on display. O Glory!

Prophecy

A sign stands in the middle of the path. It is in the center of the road. When we see it, it brings us understanding.

Prophecy

Prophecy is words from God for today. Teaching shows us the mind of God, while prophecy reveals His heart. The Scripture in the Bible gives strategy, while prophecy reveals tactics. Prophecy provides the connection between God and us, revealing His mind. It's like being on the telephone with your best friend; you can always ask His opinion on things and He gives the answer. Prophecy provides the connection to enable us to understand God's thoughts. It turns the light on.

Through prophecy, we gain an understanding of the purposes of God. It exposes sin and shows where to go. The Spirit of Council helps us. He brings council just like bumpers on the sides of a bowling alley to keep the ball going down the middle. You know those long things that they blow up and put into the gutters for little kids?

For us, the Bible, which is God's word through history, is like one of the bumpers. The other one is learning to hear His words for today. When we have both, then we are like a bowling ball going down the alley. We will be kept from going into the gutter.

Spirit of Prophecy

The spirit of prophecy among the Children of God
is like a bird that bathes in a birdbath in the garden.
God has set His bath in the garden of intimacy
with Himself. His word flutters down like
bluebirds to land in a place we have set out
in our garden. We must go from our own place
into the place where He wants us to be. Go through
the gate, tear down any walls that we have built to
keep Him out of our most private places. He wants
us to be in His most private place; His secret
garden. It is there that His words are given.
The secrets of the Kingdom are given to
Children. As the words flutter down,
they are meant to be bathed in the
bath. Seek His cleansing. Wash
the prophecy with Scripture and
internal bathing. Seek forgiveness
in any areas that you need to. Wash the words.
Maybe they are only meant for your ears alone.
It is within this garden of the intimacy of His
presence that He will tell you what to do
with them. When they are washed,
they are words sent
from
Heaven
and made ready to
sing
for others.
Sing, O Birds,
Sing of the Love of God and
His faithfulness to deliver His people!

The Prophet in the New Testament

There is a difference between the prophets in the Old Testament and in the New Testament. In I Corinthians 14, Paul says that it is his desire that we all should prophesy. Through this statement, it is evident that prophecy is not for a few select individuals. Otherwise, he would have spoken selectively to those for whom the gift was reserved.

The gift of prophecy in the New Testament is used to teach, rebuke, correct, and train in righteousness. The goal of prophecy is to draw us closer to God, direct us in purity, and help prepare us for the jobs He has for us to do while we are here on the earth. So, the goals of prophecy are the same as Scripture.

Prophecy provides the connection between hearing God's voice and understanding what is heard. We can listen to someone speak in a foreign language, but if we don't understand, the message won't get into our consciousness. By prophecy, the messages can surface to be understood by the one who needs to hear it. God is speaking through creation all the time. Why don't we hear Him? The answer is that we can't hear Him because we are missing the chip. It's like our computer will not open a program if it does not have the capability. We are missing the capability to open the messages for today from God without the gift of prophecy.

In the Old Testament, God chose specific people to be prophets. They became His mouthpiece to give messages to people. Kings that wanted to know how God felt about going to war would go to the prophet and ask. Then, the prophet would ask God, and give the answer back to the king. The King came to the prophet because he could not ask God a question and get an answer. The prophets of the Old Testament were 100% reliable. If they weren't, they were killed because God is 100% reliable and if the prophet wasn't, then his messages must not be from God.

I don't believe Paul would exhort us to all ask for the gift of prophecy, if he did not feel that it was an option. Also, God says that we don't have many things because we don't ask. I think it is a matter of asking, believing God at His word, and waiting for the answer.

There are levels of prophecy, just as there are levels of all things with God. Each level moves us closer to Him. If we receive the gift of prophecy, and can hear His voice, then, as we draw closer to Him, we should hear the whispers. At first, we can only hear His voice as He yells. Like someone with wax in our ears, the other person needs to yell to get their message across. But, then, as our ears become attuned to His voice, He doesn't need to speak as loudly to us. It's about becoming attentive to His voice.

I believe that the Holy Spirit was given to us to help us understand the things of God, including His voice. So, all of us who have been born into the family of God have the ability to hear His voice. We can ask Him a question, and He will answer. Think; what father would not answer his child when he asks a question?

And, Jesus said, that if we know how to treat our children, and give them stuff, how much more does our Father in heaven?

Learning how to hear the voice of God is about being open to Him. He does not enter where He is not welcome. We need to learn how to roll out the welcome mat and leave the door unlocked to our hearts. He wants to live in the center, and He won't tolerate any other position.

There really isn't much difference between the prophets in the Old Testament and the ones in the New Testament. God gave them messages to deliver, and they walked with them to be faithful to give them to whomever they were supposed to give them to. If Samuel was given a message for the King, he set out with it, just like one who carries the mail. We are the same. When we become faithful to hear Him and obey what He says for us to do within our own lives, then He will entrust us with more.

About three months ago, He gave me a dream telling me to get rid of my black clothes. He said that if I am to emulate the light, then I need to. So, I went into my walk-in closet and looked. It was about half full of black clothes. So, I got a bunch of trash bags and loaded up the black clothes. In the dream He gave me, He said that if I was obedient to Him, I could become a blessing to others. So, I gave them away to people that I knew needed them.

Well, two days ago, I went into my walk-in closet and was standing there, I heard His voice come into my spirit.

He said, "Sheri, I can do much more with someone obedient."

I knew what He was saying. For, I looked around, and there were still a lot of black clothes hanging in my closet. I had saved out the best ones; the angora sweaters and the formals. But, as I communed with Him while I packed them into trash bags that night, He said, "Sheri, do you want to go back to your old ways, or do you want to follow me?"

And, I said, "Lord, I want to follow you. I'm sorry that I have been disobedient."

And, I went to work the next day and gave five bags of clothes to someone who needed them. She is the same size as me and earns half as much as I do, so, I knew she probably doesn't have as nice of clothes as I do.

That night God gave me a dream. In the dream, a woman's husband dies and the very next night, she takes a new one. In between them, in the daylight, she comes to me. I am in a library room. It is like I am a bride waiting for the final piece to my gown before I am wed. She rushes in and gives me something I need. When she hands it to me, all of a sudden I am surrounded by a magnificent armor made of wire mesh. It is woven on my body as I stand there. But, the threads are woven by God. Each link is made of all of the dreams, the visions, the prayers, and the songs that I have sung to God since receiving the Holy Spirit. All of the dreams and visions, and prayers and songs flash, one by one, before my eyes, and the mail was formed by interlocking the elements by the hands of God. He knitted it from my shoulders to my toes. Then I run out of the library to my waiting vehicle. I am ready.

Of course, the next day I was eager to interpret the dream because I wanted God to knit this marvelous armor on me. So, I contemplated on it all day. Here is what I came up with:

I figure both women in the dream are me because my image of God as my husband died, and I took on His picture of who He was, the very next day. When I went into the house of His knowledge and understanding, I received what I needed to make the pieces fit.

Then, at the end of the dream, the other woman never comes out of the library. I come out, and she doesn't.

So, I asked God what it was that she brought me. For, I realize that this woman, who was me, like my old self, has brought something crucial to make the mail form. All of the mails that I have sent to Him and that He has sent to me form an armament, a covering for my body, which enables me to walk into what He has for me. What did my old self bring?

And, He answered me, "Obedience to the words I told you."

So, today I will get rid of the only black dress I saved back. It is a $250 formal. I had reasoned that, "Everybody needs a black formal."

But, after today, I realize that I am not 'everybody'. I am special and God wants me to be the light. In being the light, He will provide a new color for me for wear when I need one.

That, my friend, is moving into the gift of prophecy. Hear Him and walk into what He says with obedience. Because, when we hear Him, then obey, He will give more. His words become our covering, and we walk in that to become all He has planned for us. He has moved the things of the night (knight) into the daytime by my obedience. Throughout my life, He has brought the things hidden, to light, and they are able to walk. The dreams have taken shape and are ready to move forward, armed with things He provided.

We, as a Church, need prophetic revelation to interpret those signs leading us to the second coming of Christ. These will be provided by those who are obedient to the words they are given.

I Corinthians 12-15, II Timothy 3:16

Be Propelled

Go to God, through Jesus, by the Holy Spirit.
Run to the light, be propelled.
Awesome love shown to us times three.

Repentance

I'm sorry, dear Lord. I have neglected to obey You.
My sin cries out to me from where it hides. The
decay of my heart is rottenness to my bones.
A cancer that eats away my joy. Tare that
wretched spirit from my body, I pray.
Forgive me for my disobedience to
Your words. Selfishness, pride, and
disbelief have taken over the place where
peace and faith should reside. Your Spirit
has been kicked out, to be replaced by mine.
I have risen up. Raised up my own notions
above Yours. I have found my ways better.
My voice has become louder than Yours.
How did that happen? Where did I go
Wrong? I have wanted to follow You.
Oh, Sheri, you have, but, it's a
matter of convenience. If it
is convenient, you obey.
But, what about when
it's inconvenient?
You give, but
save some
for
yourself, just in case.
You follow My plans, but keep a
back up plan on file, in case.
Your own reasoning
has invaded your faith.
It's the flesh.
You live within it, sorry.
I know, You know I do. I was there.
But, honey, there is hope. I send it on the
wings of the Dove, I will send My relief to you.

Split Second Healing

In a split second, healing will come. The Devil will be
vanquished and we will win. Stick with Me because
we are on the winning team. In the mean time, ask
for what I have already provided for; Forgiveness
and healing. Grace and mercy. Life and healing.
Ask. Father, I ask for Your forgiveness. Thank
You that You understand. I am sorry
that I have not obeyed You all the
way. Root out my sin and help
me to bring it into the light, so
that I can become pure. Tear
out the evil from within.
Send your messengers, I pray,
because I am sick. I am in need of a
physician. Be my healer, I pray.
Father, I don't pray for
You to take away my
brokenness, but
rather, to use
it for
Your
benefit.
Those areas
that You break off, use in
other's lives. May my life bring
healing to others. Through the blood and
power of the name of Jesus I pray. Amen.

Faithful Page

It's a two AM conversation with the one I love.
Hearts melted and met.
He pages me and I put Him on it.
Be embossed and enveloped.
Be My paper to become embossed with My stamp.
Be My page to become enveloped by My presence.
A page sent from a King to a Kingdom's people
to be delivered one at a time.
A letter on the doorstep Special Delivery.
Postmarked from above from the Savior,
to serve, brought by His faithful page.

Dictation

Dictation occurs when we think
something is worth writing down.

Hummingbird

The caterpillar spins the cocoon, not forever, but for
a season. We toil and spin for our season, but soon
we will burst forth with our new wings and fly.
O winged one.
Fly. Soar, O beautiful
My heart flutters as you fly. When you fly
where I send You, it's like a hummingbird
goes from flower
to flower. I gasp with delight, glee.
You make your God to have glee, delight
to let Me provide you with My flowers. For
a bigger yard. I pray, O Lord Mine have suckle
for you to suck the nectar from. And, I will
lounge on the porch swing and watch.
And you were afraid I wouldn't
notice. I planted the flowers
and raised the hummingbird,
Why
wouldn't I notice
when they
matched?
Drink
the
pollen
and
spread
the rest.
Be like a bee, be
My honey. Be like a
bird, sing. Sing of My Honey, My
sweetness, My intimacy, The unity of your
mouth with My sweet flowers. Suckle the nectar
to deliver it somewhere else. Be My Bee. Be Mine

Dreams

There are over one hundred references to dreams in the Bible. The New Testament begins and ends with a dream. Both Mary and Joseph were visited by dreams that gave them guidance in what to do with Jesus. We, too, can gain guidance from our dreams when we learn how to unlock the messages that God has hidden within them. There are different types of dreams. (You can read *Firefly, Dreamatrix* for more information. They are books on interpretation of dreams, getting the works out of your dreams and trying to figure out what God wants you to do with them. I wrote them and you can find them through Glory Bound Books.)

There are dreams that give guidance, warning of danger, tell of sin, and the future. A dream can answer any question that we want to ask God. I know, because I do it. With me, when I have a question, I ask God, and He usually gives me four dreams in the same night. But, remember, friend, that I have been faithful to write them down. If you desire God to answer questions through dreams, you need to become faithful to write them down in the middle of the night and bring them back to Him for interpretation.

Examples in the Bible.
In Daniel 2:3, Nebuchadnezzar had a dream. He was the king of the time and became anxious to understand the dream. He knew that He must interpret the dream because it was telling him how to run the kingdom. If we follow the story, he found Joseph, who interpreted the dream. With the interpretation, he made plans to help the kingdom get through a drought. He believed the dream and acted on it averting a problem.

Joseph knew what to do, because God gave Him a dream to interpret Nebuchadnezzar's dream. But, Joseph, did not become a dream expert overnight. He had dreams at a young age that told him of future events. He knew about things because he paid attention to the dreams. He copied them and brought them to God to help him with them. (Genesis 37).

Jacob's ladder, and Peter's trance, along with the book of Revelation are all indications that God speaks through dreams and visions into our minds to direct us and give us His voice.

Another Joseph in the New Testament, had several dreams telling him what to do with Mary and Jesus. They told him how to avert Herod who would seek to destroy Jesus. The dreams provided him with guidance. (Matt 1:21).

Remember, Harod's wife had a dream when Jesus was on trial? The dream said that Jesus was a pure man and had done no wrong. I believe this dream was from God.

How do you suppose God gave the instructions to build the Ark of the Covenant? I bet He used the pad of the mind of Moses to draw on. The Bible says that it was the finger of God that inscribed the 10 commandments, but what about the rest?

Dreams are pictures in our minds given at night when we are asleep. God speaks to us in several ways. When we pray, God promises to answer us. When He does, often, we don't recognize it because it comes to us like a foreign language. We need to interpret it for it to make sense of it to us. It is like we are on one shore, and we can see where we want to be across the channel of water. We are looking for a bridge that will get us there. God has not provided a bridge. He has provided a channel with a ferry boat. We have to get on the boat and trust Him to direct us down the channels that He has for us. This is the channel of His love. The boat is the vehicle of communication that He has provided through the Holy Spirit.

Dreams are riddles that have to be solved to get the answers. They provide direction, teaching, confirmation, and encouragement directly from God. There is no middle man, no preacher. They are God's word given to us individually. And, everybody dreams.

Often, we don't see the dreams as messages from God because we don't fathom His Love for us and His constant desire to be in our lives.

He comes into our world in unusual ways. He uses pictures we can relate to. He has a lot of things to choose from, but our world limits Him. I see dreams in this way, suppose we were humans, and wanted to raise an ant family. We needed to send messages so that they know what to do to make things go smoothly.

We have to use things that they understand to communicate with them. In the same way God uses dreams for us. When He wants to tell us about Himself, He puts our 'father' in the dream. When He wants to give us a message about our 'brethren', He uses our brothers and sisters. If we have a dream about a house, it could be us, for we are the temple of God. Get it?

The interpretation of dreams does not replace the Scriptures. It is separate. They are pictures that help us to understand the truths of God. We are to be careful not to spend all our time on them instead of studying the Word of God.

Through the ages God has spoken to people through individuals who became His 'mouthpiece'. He would put words into their mouth and send them to speak to groups of people to get them to follow His ways. These individuals were consecrated (set apart) and anointed (given special ability) to do whatever mission God wanted them to do. Moses, Aaron, Jeremiah, Isaiah, John the Baptist were prophets. They were sent for God to communicate His voice to people.

After all the prophets came, God sent His Son, Jesus, to solve the problem once and for all. Jesus Christ is God's Word revealed to mankind in the flesh. He shows us who God is. He is the very voice of God Himself. Jesus became the message IN Himself apart from human messengers (Prophets). The Word continues to speak to us today because Jesus has Eternal Character and does not change.

Dreams mix creation with the Word of God to help us understand Him better. We are stuck in our world, and He understands this. We cannot move, so He does. He uses language we understand and mixes it with our life experiences to help us know how He feels.

A dream is similar to the Word of God. It is words of God. It pierces between our soul and spirit. When our will has been submitted to Him, and our flesh is asleep, it is a perfect time for Him to talk to us.

We do not have any of the distractions of the daytime schedule. He has us in a position where we don't have a choice of whether or not to listen to Him. The dream is like a message on the end of a sword. When our flesh is asleep and our will is submitted to Him, then He can commune our spirit with His Holy Spirit to send us clear messages. We become open and broken and the message pierces through.

When we sleep, our flesh is silent. Our stomach cannot tell us it is hungry because we are not awake to listen to it. If our mind is committed to the purposes of God, our will does not get in the way, either. Only our spirit is awake. It is an open path for God to write on the screen of our mind with His pictures.

Message of the Dream

The message of the dream should move us closer to God because that is the goal of God in all of His interactions with us. The dream might reveal areas of sin. If we have been praying for God to reveal some hidden sin in our life, perhaps He will give us a dream (Psalms 51). Maybe there needs to be a change in our life. Perhaps we are off the track that God wants us to be on. He will, often, reveal this to people in dreams. If we are in a position of authority, God often will speak to us about individuals whom are under our authority. This will provide direction on what to do with them to help them to move closer to Him.

Another area where God talks to individuals through dreams is with "Strongholds". Strongholds are areas in our lives of bad teaching where have learned something wrongly, and God is trying to tell us to relearn it His way.

Dreams may be prophetic, insight to provide direction to decisions for the future. They also provide heart direction if your heart needs to be realigned to God. The direction may be immediate or lifelong.

Remember that dreams are like boxes to be delivered to our doorstep. They have stickers on the other side of the box.

This means that if we had a dream several years ago, there is another message if we ask God to turn it over again.

We can revisit each dream time and time again. A dream may be timely with a message, but it also has a bigger message for another time. Only a message from God could do that!

146

How to come up with God's Message:

It is important to not try to interpret the dream from any other source than the Bible and God Himself. I do not interpret other's dreams. I can't. No one can. I can, however, ask questions, that if the individual answers, will lead to the meaning of the dream.

I will show you:

First, write down the dream. A dream is like a piece of art. If you stand too close, then you can't see the whole picture. If you have an empty notebook nearby the bed at night, then you will be more likely to write them down. Jesus said that if we are faithful in a little, then He will give more. If He gives you dreams and you do not write them down, then why would He give more?

One of the reasons, I am sure that I have so many dreams, is that I have made an effort to write them down and find out their meanings. I have many dreams, however, that I have not written down and still more that I wrote down, but have never figured out. Dreams are mysteries that need to be unraveled by the Word of God and the presence of the Holy Spirit.

After you write down the dream, step back. Often times, He plays on words. Sea doesn't mean the ocean but see. A father in a dream can mean your real father or the Father in Heaven. A sister could mean your sister in the flesh, or it could mean your brethren at church. I use a dictionary to help me expand my thinking. I write each word on a piece of paper and try to think of as many meanings as possible for the words.

A locked door in your dream may cause you to think about an entrance in your life that is 'locked'. Dreams are metaphorical.

You need to expand your mind. It is a matter of starting to think outside of your box. It is the beginning to learning to think using the mind of Christ.

Next, ask God about the true message of the dream. He will guide and help if you ask Him. Take the written details of the dream and look up the words in the Bible

Some of the weirdest dreams have become the most profound, for me, when I took them back to Him. The first time I had a naked dream, I was worried that Satan had entered my dreams. So I asked. What He said is that my nakedness within the dream simply shows that I am willing to be open with Him. I am naked, just like when I was born. It is not a bad thing to God.

Allow Him to give meaning to the dream apart from human language. For example, In the Bible, Jesus is called a door, and individuals go 'through' Him. Try to take the language out of the symbols of the dream and allow them to be interpreted by God's viewpoint. Many Bibles have cross-references to verses that can add understanding to passages. Read these for additional insight into meanings.

A concordance is helpful. It is a book, similar to a dictionary, which has words listed in the Bible. It is usually found in the back of a Bible and the words are listed alphabetically. It gives a reference in the Bible where a verse can be found with that word in it.

Sit quietly and ask questions to God. Have paper and pen ready to copy His answers. I take my dreams to the desert hiking with me and talk to God. I ask Him questions and copy the answers. I used to take an index card. Now I take a notebook.

Once, when I had a dream that I could not figure out, God intervened in a special way. There were crabs in the dream. I don't care how much you tear the Bible apart; there are no crabs in it.

So, I was perplexed about what those were. I had pretty much constrained myself to think that they were evil things lurking in dark places eating trash.

Two weeks after I had the dream, I was met by a friend in the hall. She was a work acquaintance who I did not really know. But, she stopped me dead in the hall and said, "Sheri, I had a dream last night. You and I were at bar eating crabs all night."

Well, I was even more stumped. To think I was eating these evil things lurking!

So, I went back to God and the Bible with the new piece that she provided. It led me to the answer of the dream. The crabs did represent sin.

So, I went to the woman who had the dream, and I confessed to her that her dream had interpreted mine. So, I asked her if she would like my dream to be used to interpret hers.

She came to my house, and I did both dreams side by side. They formed a beautiful picture of how Jesus provides forgiveness for our sins. Her side of the dream related to how He forgives us once and for all. Mine was on how He forgives all other sins on a continuing basis.

She prayed with me and turned her life over to God at my kitchen table that morning at seven AM over a box of donuts. Don't underestimate the power of dreams.

Fly Freely

God is releasing prophecy. He will sing into our hearts
as we turn them over to His control. He has removed
the hindrances that have held us in. We are meant
to fly freely, not be put in a place,
watered, fed and tended by a man.
We are not parrots, but blue
birds,
love birds,
swans, and humming
birds. That which
could not sing
before
was
in a cage.
A bird taught
to parrot, now sings.
Sing!
O birds, sing! Your Savior has Risen!
Wisdom Teams. Wisdom is found in a place
teeming with life. The words enter and change you.

Dumb

I was dumb and He released me. Like soap slipping into the
bathtub, I thought I would do it myself. But, He did it. We all
have dreams. They go all slippery and sliding into the tub. I
should have known, I was going to fall. The eyes of my
heart, He has opened. His voice, I now hear. And, I can't
keep quiet about the miracle He has done
He took someone who was dumb and completely
healed her. He took my life, after my dreams
had slid from my fingers, and slid His arms
of Salvation
around me.
My dreams have slid into His.
I'll send a note down;
Some give and others withhold.
They refuse to open their hand to anyone else.
Their Teacher has come, but they didn't recognize Him.
They are
dumb.
There is a
little searchlight.
It works like a beam in our
hand, day and night. It can't be seen
from the side. It must
be a light that is
directed
with a hand. And, He has chosen
to use ours. May they see the light, Dear
Lord, Open their eyes, their heart, and their ears
to hear Your voice, see Your face, and know Your heart.

Your Antenna

Where's your antenna? On the roof or in your heart?
In your head, or with God above? Center the
radar dish to pick up My signal. It's
the Christian Station. Full
Gospel 24-7. 24 hours
a day, 7 days a week.

Copy

We need to take
note of what He tells
us. Copy the answer. He is
the Word and has been given to us.
He is the answer, so when we realize which
aspect of His character we need to emulate, then copy.

Word Flutters

Birds bathe in the birdbath that we set in the garden
for them. God's word to us flutters down like
bluebirds to land on the place we have
set out in our garden. The words to
us are baptized in the bath,
washed and made ready
to sing for others.

Wondrous Signs

Wondrous signs from God above sent down to the one I love.
A signpost holds a speed sign. It also holds a yield sign.
There's a stop sign, and a merge one, too.
Different times in our lives.
God gives us instruction.
Go share the gospel.
Stop remembering your sins. Yield to My grace.
Merge with My Son because He stepped out of Heaven
and stopped in. He yielded His will to the Father, set His
life as an example for us. He desires us to merge, join in;
become one with Him; To get on the same freeway that He
has provided through His blood. He sped up to allow us to
slow down. Grace after grace freely given. Only, we need
to stop going our own way and yield onto His free way.
Learn to keep pace with the pacer car,
Jesus,
who
has
gone
before.
Keep our
eyes focused on
the road. Don't get
distracted; avert the exit ramps;
bypass other's ways. Take the road that
leads to the high way of His eternal righteousness.

Genesis

We are approaching a genesis; a new world. Open our eyes, Lord, that we may see our new world, the wonders of Your new creation.

Visions

A vision is a mental representation of something that is not tangent. You can't reach out and touch it. Often, when we pray for another person, we may have a symbolic vision that comes up into our mind. It may be a scene, or a thing, or a person (rarely). There are many individuals in the Bible that had visions or trance states.

In Acts 10 Cornelius has a vision in which God tells him to accept Paul and pray over him to receive his sight again. Each of the books of Prophecy in the scriptures are either visions or dreams. Jeremiah, Ezekiel, and Revelation all are written like someone who is on drugs. They are all visionary and prophetic. Often, God speaks to us in an unconventional manner. We need to be open to listen to Him. *God is not limited by our refusal to accept the visions and pray into them, we only limit our access to information that will help us with the answer.* He will only use willing vessels. Visions can give direction to prayer.

The Scripture is not silent on the subject of dreams and visions. God says, *"He who has a dream let him tell it, He who has my word speak it faithfully. What does straw have to do with wheat? Is not my word a fire and a hammer that breaks the rock into pieces?* (Jeremiah 23:28-30).

Visions and dreams are not the Word of God. They must be taken to the Word to be interpreted. There they will find their foundation. Once the foundation is built, then the building can progress the direction of the dream or vision.

They are active prayer

Visions are visual messages from God that need to be interpreted to be useful. They are pictures put into our mind. They are one of the ways God talks back to us, so they come to us while in prayer. To have visions, we must be focused on God. He can talk to us only when we are open to receive the answer. Only then will God be able to talk into our minds.

Hebrews 10:16 says, "This is the covenant that I will make with them: After those days, says the Lord: I will put My laws upon their heart, and on their mind I will write them."

We are called to take every thought captive to the obedience of Christ. The vision must be weeded out from other thoughts that are going through our mind. We must rid our mind of distractions when we pray. We should schedule prayer times and make them uninterrupted time where we talk to God and listen. It's about learning to be still before God.

When Elijah ran up to the cave to escape Jezebel, God said He wanted to talk to Him. Elijah recognized God's voice because it was in the 'gentle blowing' wind, not the storm. God wasn't in the great and strong wind, the earthquake, or the fire. If we follow that story, Elijah just waited for things to quiet down, then, he went out to meet God. Sometimes, we need to wait for our own lives to quiet down, so we can listen.

The vision is a picture. It is similar to one on the wall. For instance, there is a picture of a pathway with a bridge. To pray 'into' a vision, we must picture ourselves within the picture. We would walk on the pathway and cross the bridge. (God provides a pathway, the bridge is Jesus Christ). So, to use a vision, take the picture and bring it back to God. Bring it to His world for the interpretation. He lives within the Scriptures and within the Holy Spirit.

Take a look at the scriptures and see how the vision correlates with the person in their environment. When asked to pray for a baby, we may have a vision of tiny lever blinds. This message from God speaks about 'blinds' that became opened. We can use the concordance and find many examples of people who were 'blind' and God shone the light into their situation. If we relate it to the situation of prayer, we can see where God wants to shine His light on that baby or on the family through the face of the baby. I would pray both those ways. It doesn't hurt to pray more than you need to.

Here are some examples:

1) One of the visions that I had was of little trees growing in little pots on the stairs of the altar in the sanctuary.

I researched the Bible and saw that God desires to make us to be a church that plants seedlings. We are to be planted in good soil. So to build on this foundation, I looked up Isaiah 61 and prayed it into our Church. I also prayed Matthew 13 where Jesus talks about the seed being planted. I prayed all of the verses that I could find on seedlings.

2) When I prayed for my husband, once, I had a vision of a plow. I searched the scriptures and found verses with the word 'plow' in them. Then I prayed these character traits in to His life. I could see that God wanted him to be one that sows the Word and one that helps to prepare individuals to receive the Good News of Jesus.

3) The vision is meant to direct the prayer. We need to allow it to do this. For example; we may have a vision of a clam shell with a pearl inside. The clam is shut tight. This vision should direct us to pray 'pearl' stuff. We can pray that the individual will 'open up' to whatever God has for him.

There can be progressive visions, as well. If God is teaching you something, then, He will show one thing, and add to it later. I have had visions of a problem, then, as I continue praying, I have a vision of the 'fix'.

For example, if I am praying for someone and I have a vision of an uprooted plant, I continue to pray Scripture and in tongues until God reveals a vision that is a positive one because I know that from James, an uprooted tree is a symbol of a Christian who is without roots. That is a problem which needs help. So, I continue to pray through the problem to the solution.

To me, when God gives a negative vision, He is telling me of a problem that needs to be fixed. He wouldn't give it to me without a reason. So, I dig around in the Scriptures for the answer to whatever the problem is, then, pray it in.

For the uprooted tree, I would pray the Scriptures about being rooted and grounded in the love of Christ and I Corinthians 13 which is all about learning to love. Sometimes, there can be a progression of a vision. God may show us an individual in a bad condition, such as in an animal trap, and we know that He needs to become released from the trap. We can pray 'release' verses. There are verses about how God releases us from the bondage's of Satan. With this vision, we may have another vision; one of release, when the individual is 'prayed through'.

Praying into visions is like doing math. God gives the problem, then it is up to us to come up with the answer. He will help along the way, but it is our mouth that prays His will into action. He is breath, we provide the air. He is the movement; we provide the willingness to be used. He moves the spiritual realms when we speak His words.

It is by our mouth and our heart that His heart is moved, Satan is kicked out of situations, and His Kingdom is moved forward. When you are praying in a group, as you pray, allow each one to call out their vision. The others can help to find Scripture to help back the vision. Then, each prays in the Scripture that they contribute to the group.

You continue to pray until you reach the answer. It will be given, and you all will know that it is the one that you have been seeking. Just like math, there is only one answer when God asks the question; His answer. He has the answers written down in the back of the book. Just ask. They are in revelations of His mind which are given to our hearts as they are open to His.

I Kings 19:12, Isaiah 61:11, Matthew 13.46, II Corinthians 10:5

Hidden Head Lights

Dream:

There is a car with pop up headlights. The engine is turned on and the lights are on but they are turned down (in). There is power, but the lights are turned inward.

Interpretation:

How do we make our light point inward? The light isn't to direct us, but to provide direction to the vehicle He has provided for our ministry.

He isn't here to tell us what to do, but what to do with what He has given us. It's not an outward direction, but an inward direction. Motivation will direct us. When we are motivated by the love of God for others, we will be directed in all of our steps because they can't be wrong. Whether we step to the right or the left, people will be blessed through the ministry God has given us. Let the ministry direct.

God will reveal His will to us from His Holy Spirit into our heart. Our spirit needs to be taught how to listen to our heart as it communes with God. We need to value what God is teaching us. Write those words down and ask Him what they mean. Only He can interpret what He has put on our hearts. Ask for wisdom and understanding. God has provided us a window through a relationship with Jesus Christ to know His ways for us.

Our mind needs to be taken out of the loop. He will not reveal His will for us to our mind. What God tells our hearts to do will provide the illumination to us. It makes us shine with His light.

God is the one who enlightens us; we don't have to try to do it on our own. Just ask Him. It only takes as long as it does for us to blink, for God to reveal His vision to us. It is like shutting our eyes then opening them again. When we open them again, we see with His sight, not our own.

Our heart needs to be pure for God to shine His glorious light into it. If our heart is the screen that He writes on, then if it is not white, the light won't shine on it very well. We cannot allow anything to impede this purity. We must get rid of anything that blocks the light. When He points out sin in our lives, we need to take care of it. Then, listen closely to His words. We must guard the purity of God's words in our hearts and do not mix them with impure thoughts.

Everyone has hearts with eyes. The eyes of their heart see into our eyes. Like two cars meeting; our headlights flash at one another. When our eyes shine with the love of God to others, they will see Him as they look into our eyes. The Holy Spirit that God has instilled in us will be seen when we look at them. God shines with His love, as we love others by using the ministry He has given us.

When we get the eyesight that God has intended, He will make our steps to be faithful to His plan. He never gets tired of providing us with His direction and the empowerment to do it. When we look to Him, the path will seem like we aren't even touching the ground. No rocks will make us stumble. We won't get tired because He will continue to renew us with His strength.

Following His voice within our heart will continue to inspire us in His direction. This will provide direction to others as well.

Genesis 3:5, Psalms 19:8, 119:18, Proverbs 4:20-25, 7:2, 15, Isaiah 29.10, 40.26, 52.8-15, Matthew 5.29, Luke 11:34, I Corinthians 2:9, 15:52, Ephesians 1:18, 6:6, Colossians 3:22.

Types of Prophecy

As I have studied the subject of prophecy through the Scriptures and by asking God, I have noted that there are several types. I have outlined them below. It is evident that God does not have plans for each of us to have the same gifting, so how is it different? It's not that one is better than the next, but rather, that one is more of a pure gift. It's sort of like horses. Some are bred for races, and others are bred for trail riding. A few are bred for both. God has those with the gifting of prophecy in several areas. Just because a person says that he is a 'prophet' and can say words for the whole congregation, doesn't mean that there are not others within the same Church who are not also prophets. It just means that their gifting is prophecy with a different focus.

What I have noticed is that it seems like God has placed us on different hills overlooking the same kingdom. One person may be able to see further than another, but they are all looking at the same city. One person may have prophetic gifting with a tendency toward words for a country, and another with words for a city. One may speak to those who need salvation and another to those who need healing. The ones with multiple gifting, like healing, may have a mixture, and be able to do both. Just like the horse, I was talking about.

Testimonial prophecy:

One type of prophecy is telling our testimony of Jesus' work within our lives. When we live on the earth and have the power of the Holy Spirit flowing through us, there will be a constant stream of testimony on how God is working in our lives to bring about His Kingdom. It is interpreting for others, events in our lives, as they relate to God, rather than us, only. If we see a miracle, we tell others. We give the glory to God for what He is doing. We are interpreting His actions for others.

One dream God gave me on this was about my going into an office and gathering up the left over popcorn that others weren't eating. I gathered it up. After I gathered it up, they noticed that they didn't have any. So, they started to come to me, wanting some. God sends us miracles on a daily basis and often, we do not recognize them.

These individuals had taken His 'popped freshness' for granted. I didn't. I gathered it up. When I gathered it up, they noticed it because when I redistributed it with the seal of God. I sent it back with oil and salt. It's the Holy Spirit given at the right season (oil and salt.)

This type of prophecy is when the words of God well up within us. We feel the Holy Spirit prompting us to say something to someone at a specific time. It is the 'word' which brings encouragement and helps to motivate others to move closer to God.

Recently, when I was visiting a church, I ended up in a Sunday school class where they were studying I Corinthians. They skipped over the 12th chapter calling it irrelevant. I could feel the prompting of the Spirit rising within my chest. My heart started to beat faster and faster. I knew that He wanted me to tell them that I had prayed in tongues for their Church all night. He wanted me to tell them about the power in praying in tongues with interpretation. But this Church didn't believe that way, so I stalled. I reasoned that I didn't know any of these people and they would surely think that I was crazy. Well, my heart kept beating faster and faster. I know it was God because I reached a point where I had to either tell them or have a heart attack in the chair.

So, I took a deep, ragged breath and interrupted the instructor, telling him how the gifts of the Holy Spirit are for today. And, furthermore, I had used them to pray for their Church this morning. Then, I went on to tell them how I had prayed specific things for their lives that God had shown me that morning.

You could hear a pin drop in the place. This congregation does not believe in speaking in tongues.

They view it as fanaticism and think it is faked. So, to have me tell them that I had prayed for their families in tongues, brought a lot of confusion to the class. What happened was that the instructor followed me around for two days afterward listening to my prayers. It opened a door that had not been opened in his life. God wanted to widen his views using my testimony.   *Revelation 12.11*

The Gift of Prophecy

This is a spiritual gift that brings with it the ability to help others see God within their situations where they haven't seen Him before. It turns the light on. This gift is often accompanied by the Word of Knowledge, Word of Wisdom, discernment, and understanding.

The Word of Knowledge is information given to someone that they would have no way of knowing without God telling him. It is knowledge about something or someone that God provides. It is current events.

The Word of Wisdom is information given to someone that he would have no way of knowing without God telling him, as well. It is what God wants the person to do about the problem. It is the word of God; Scripture that provides God's mind into the situation. He has the answer and it is found through seeking God's wisdom. A person with the gift of Wisdom will tell others God's mind in the situation. He will have a verse. It is always substantiated in the Scriptures. Someone who claims to have the Word of Wisdom and is not able to find a verse to substantiate it, needs to be taken with caution. Many times we don't know what gifts we have. So, sometimes we claim the wrong gifting just because we aren't sure, but know that we have something.

Remember, that the Fear of the Lord is the beginning of wisdom, so the fear of the Lord should be evident within the ministry of the individual who has the gift of Wisdom. This person loves God so much, it oozes out all over the place. When it oozes out, he spills onto others as the gift.

The gift of knowledge is different. Knowledge is about events. Someone with the gift of knowledge may have indications from God related to future events. Or, he may have words from God on things today. But, they are not Scriptures, they are things present. Someone with the gift of knowledge can tell events of lives, and injuries, etc. With this gift, he could call out the need for you to be healed of a specific ailment. He only knows this information because God has told him. Now, he needs the gift of Wisdom to know how God wants to move within your life to bring about healing.

Wisdom provides the how and why of stuff, whereas Knowledge provides the what.

Let's suppose someone who is speaking from the pulpit proclaims that God wants to heal anyone in the congregation with a back injury. He calls on those with back injuries to come forward. That is the word of Knowledge.

So, you have a back injury, so you go forward. Now, there are 100 people at the front of the Church, so the speaker asks for help to pray over them all.

Now, your friend, Sally, comes to you and she lays her hand on you. Then, she prays, "Lord, In Your Word You claim that You will heal all who come to You. You have said that we are healed by Your stripes. Please heal my friend. "

Sally has just used the gift of Wisdom because the Holy Spirit brought the verse to mind and the power of God moved within her to pray it into action. She was moved within the spirit of prophecy with word of Wisdom.

There are 'hearers' and there are 'seers' within the Prophetic realm. God comes to prophets two ways. One way He comes is that He plays a 'video' in their mind. It may be a vision or a dream. He also comes to Prophets with His voice. He may 'whisper' into their spirit or He may speak audibly. Both avenues are through God's heart into the heart of the Prophet. It is His Spirit to their spirit that the messages are communicated.

Consequently, the more open to God we are, the more we will be able to hear Him.

Forth telling is declaring the word of the Lord, communicating the heart of God for today. This word can be brought through teaching, preaching, the spoken prophetic word, vision and interpretation and symbolic acts. Many times singing can be really prophetic. It is just the song that is needed. Anyone that gives us a 'word' that we need right now, is forth telling with a demonstration of the gift of prophecy.

A lot of art is prophetic. I have included quite a bit within the books that I have written. It communicates the heart of God on paper in a form that speaks to our heart.

Another aspect of the prophetic role is **predictive prophecy**, called foretelling. This has to do with knowing the future as it is perceived in the heart and mind of God. Sometimes, God tells us the future to encourage us. Other times, He gives us a glimpse of it to warn us. Dreams can be a predictive prophecy. They may warn us or lead us into future events.

In the New Testament, Paul exhorts everyone to look toward being a prophet; to come to understand God's words for today. We start with learning who He is. There is an interaction between Knowledge of God and Wisdom from God. Knowledge is about who He is; what does He like, what has He done in the past. This is found in the Bible.

Wisdom is about knowing Him as a person. We can know all about Him without knowing Him personally, just as we may know a movie star through reading about Him, but never know the individual. When we know Him on a personal level, we will know what His desires are for us and others. It's about pressing into the relationship with Him. He wants to tell us His mind, but He must be able to trust us with the information. If we are faithful in few things, He will give us more. A Prophet is one who is faithful to deliver a message to others.

Prophecy does the same things that the Word of God does because it is the word of God for today given to His people. It encourages, comforts, provides direction, releases vision and calling, exposes the enemy, shows the Kingdom of God values and helps to prepare the Children of God for the return of Christ. Their goal is to build the Church to become unified with Christ.

I Corinthians 12-14, Ephesians 4, Colossians 1,
II Timothy 3.16, Revelation 2-5.

Healing

Healing
comes as
we walk down
the middle of the road to His voice.
The road is the road to Holiness. As we walk
toward His voice, we walk toward the avenue
of becoming
built
into His
righteousness
here on earth.
Miracles happen.
Heaven touches earth..

Amazing Love

E're He found me, I was lost.
He knew where I was all the time.
I was blind.
Amazing love healed my eyes,
opened the eyes of my heart
to see His amazing love.

Healing on His Wings

As He is lifted, we are too. It's about soaring with the
Holy Spirit in the new things of God. Being lifted on
His voice. Risen with Christ; merging with Him and
being made in His likeness anew. Go to the throne
and pick up your wings. Belt them with truth across
your chest; Across your heart. Climb a mountain
and step out by faith to enter the updraft of the
wind of His voice. Prepare to test the wind.
Know the direction of it, then, step into
that direction. Your provision is through
His voice. He is the foundation, the ground.
It is not done by our feet, but by our spirit.
Not by flesh, but by Spirit. There is
a constant current of wind.
Just as the River
of
Life
through
the voice of God
flows
everlasting.
If you can't tell which
way the wind is blowing, how
can you know where to launch the glider?
We find God by following His voice to Him

Dropped Baby

Dream:

I was in the Operating Room of a hospital and responsible for the delivery of the baby. I don't see the mother. When the baby is born, someone drops it face down next to the table. I couldn't see if it was OK. I gather it up and check it, put it on the table. I give it what it needs. Then, I turn on the lights.

Interpretation:

The baby is a vision given to someone for something God wants to do within the Kingdom of God. People drop their 'baby' because they can't see it. Our role is to help others find their babies.

A Painted Window

There is a window in this house that has not been
opened for years. In fact, they forgot it opens.
They have painted it shut. It's a window
to heaven. A window of our heart to the Lord's.

X Ray Vision

God has been watching over you and is supervising
to make sure His plans are fulfilled. You don't
need to fear the enemy who would like to
destroy the plans that He has given you.
He does not just give you plans then
walk away.
He helps to build the house.
He follows you along the
route. He is your friend.
He becomes your
intimate friend
and whispers into your ear
as you listen to His voice all of
the details to fulfill His mission.
And, He shows His love to you
over and over along the
way. He will give
you X ray
vision.
You will see through to
the goals when you join with Him.

Open Heart

Only when we are able to close our eyes to
the ways of the world and open our
spiritual eyes to the Holy Spirit, can we begin to
see the words that God wants to tell us.
His messages come through an
open door within our heart.
The words are written
on the back of
our eyelids.
Close
our
eyes
and
open our heart.
He lives within parked
on the edge of the sea. The
boat is attached with a chain.

Geyser Vision

This one is a vision:
There is a geyser. It is aqua blue and bubbly. I have an underwater camera view. There are trees along the banks with their roots extended into the water. They are different kinds; spruce, redwood, and pine; All tall and beautiful, green and stately. There are many small trails leading through the trees to the water. The water has, what looks like chemical deposits along the bank. It looks like calcium deposits because there is discoloration along the shore.

"The water is alive and happy to have found a place to release the pressure."

Interpretation:
God wants to release His power and presence among His children. He needs us to become willing to be open to Him. The water is His Holy Spirit. The trees are Christians of many varieties.

The trails are individual trails that each one of us must walk down to get to where we are supposed to be within our gifting. Our gifting must join with the presence of the Holy Spirit.

We wash in the water of the Word. The chemical deposits are the 'hardness' of our heart that we leave at the water.

Isaiah 42-47

Mysterious Diner

The Dream:

The family is together, and they are making a large meal to eat for a holiday. Someone comes to the door. He is persistent in getting in. I go from one door to the next, trying to keep him out. I chase him around in the yard to try to get rid of him. He is mellow, but persistent on wanting into the house. He pushes against the sliding glass door, and it falls off the track completely. He gets in because others open the door. I wrestle him down to the floor and start to beat him up. He continues to be passive. Someone gets down on their hands and knees and looks him in the face.

Then, the intruder says, "I am praying for Her," Referring to me.

When I stop, I realize he does not mean to hurt; he merely wants to become part of the party. He's foreign. Then I introduce him to the others at the party. He asks to take off his outer garment. He is very colorful underneath. We all sit down. They are very hungry. When we pass the meat, they take a lot. It doesn't look like we will have enough for everyone, but the mother brings us more. I carry a dish.

It is a sweet dish with marshmallows on top. When I set it on the table, it rolls down. It has wheels. I learn to turn it so the wheels are facing the other direction. Someone has said grace. The mysterious intruder has joined us for supper.

Interpretation:

Often that which we work the hardest to keep out is that which God has sent to dine with us.

Power in our Voice

There is power in our voice. It is the power to move
God. When we call, He answers. When He answers,
He brings Himself.
He is not like a busy father who merely mumbles
'what', yet does not stop His own activities to
see what the child needs.
It is like He stops what He is doing: Which
is waiting for us to call, and gives His
full attention to the movement of our
hearts
toward His. This is what He has
been waiting for. Like someone
adding up the budget, He has
been waiting for
it to balance out. It
is a balance in
our desire
to
want
to be
with Him
as much as He
wants to be with us. Our
voice moves God because it is His
plan to teach us behavior by demonstration.

Questions for the builder

What do the stones look like, that build the walls of the
Kingdom of God? We are to be shaped by the potter
to be able to be put into the wall. Only after we
have been shaped by Him, can we fit into the
spot He has for us in the wall. How do
we know where we belong? A stone has
to be shaped so that it will fit into that
spot that He has for us. How do you
shape a stone? You can take a rotor
saw, but it's much easier to be given
a stone that is the right size. No tools
are to be used at the site of the building
when the wall is put together. The stones
are lifted by the builder
and put into place. He puts them into
the place they need to be. He needs
to get close to them, reach out
to them, and elevate them
from the place
where they
were to
a place
they
need
to be.
That is
why when we
are set in the
place we
belong
on the wall, we see everything
from the perspective He has put us in.
We can't see the other side of the wall, but
He has others there. That is why it is important
everyone takes their place. The wall protects the houses.

Prophecy Shared

The Church gets side tracked when they read 'Builder Bob' cut out instructions.

Thunder in the Word

Dream: *God's voice is like thunder*

Interpretation:
Our spiritual eyes must be opened to see the light. But it is the voice that tells us how close His power is to us. When a storm comes, the wind has a sudden rush; then, the sky becomes darkened. We can hear the thunder in the distance. When we hear the voice of God, then it should cause us to look up into the heavens, like looking for a storm. We look up to see when the rain will come. When we hear the voice of God, then, we look up to see His display of power and His shower of power into our lives.

We cannot direct thunder anymore than we can direct God's voice. The power is displayed in the ability to illuminate, to enlighten, to set afire our souls to Him. It is pure current that always strikes our highest structure and goes to the ground. We reach out to Him using His rod (the Word of God) longing for His power strike. When He does, He always goes to our foundation. If we are founded IN Christ, then the building is secure.

His rod of righteousness must be outstretched atop the building to have the power hit it as the tallest object. We need to train our ears to hear His voice and anticipate the power of God coming to us in the form of lightning. We lift up His Word, hold it up above our heads, and look for Him to come along and flow through us with His current. Our foundation has to be built on our relationship with the firm Rock, Jesus.

Thunder in the Scriptures is associated with the Voice of God coming to people. It is always a group of people. The thunder is usually accompanied by hail, lightning, and often a trumpet. Exodus 9:23 Moses stretched out his hand in Egypt, and God sent hail, thunder, and lightening to open the way for freedom into the promised land. In Exodus 20:18, when God gave the ten commandments, there was thunder, lightning, a trumpet, and a mountain smoking.

God was attempting to open a way to Himself for the people, but they did not recognize His voice and were afraid.

Why didn't Moses have any problem going into the cloud?

He knew Who the cloud represented. He recognized the voice of God as representing a loving God. He knew the character of God well enough to know God was into life, not death. He had experienced spirit to Spirit contact with God, and his hunger for God's Spirit led him into the cloud. He knew that God wanted to be with him, and his desire was to be with God. The others were kept away from God because of 'fear of Death.'

In I Samuel 7:10, the people go to Samuel, and Samuel goes to God. Samuel offers sacrifice to God, and while He is sacrificing, God thunders and throws the enemies into a panic. Samuel opens the way to God, and God opens the way for the people to win a battle.

Again, in I Samuel 12:18, Samuel called on God to send rain, thunder, and lightening. All the people stood in awe of God and Samuel. They had asked for a king. Samuel opens the way to God, then God opens the way to kingship.

When the Lord points His affection at us, it is overwhelming. He holds nothing back. His voice thunders in marvelous ways. He does great things beyond our understanding, so we can tell the difference between Him and others. It is His voice that touches our hearts. For He is the one that unleashes the lightning beneath the whole heaven.

He gets ready to talk, there are rumbles in the spiritual kingdom, like the ruffling of the water before a wave. Then, He brings enlightenment. After that comes the thunder of His majestic voice. He shakes us, breaks us, twists us, and brings us down to ground level with His voice. His voice strikes our groundwork.

In Job 38 The Lord answered Job out of the storm. Job had darkened God's counsel with words without knowledge. He had listened to others when He should have been consulting God on the subject. God points out men do not know the laws of the heavens. Only God alone.

Then, when God sends His voice within the thunder, Job says, 'My ears had heard of You, but now my eyes have seen You.'

The thunder enlightens us to His voice. It opens us up enough to hear Him. God raises His voice to the clouds and covers Himself with a flood of water. He sends lightning bolts and has them report to Him, 'Here we are.'

God knows where His voice is at all times. His voice goes out, and He follows it to bring about its purposes. God opens our hearts to hear Him and opens our minds to understand His voice.

When we cry to God, He answers us out of the brightness of His presence. He brings hailstones and lightening to scatters and routs enemies. The valleys are exposed and the foundations are laid bare at the blast of the breath of His nostrils. Then, He reaches down, gathers us up, and draws us out of deep waters. He rescues because He delights in us.

The voice of the Lord breaks the cedars. He shakes the desert, twists the oaks, strips the forests bare. Then, when He has cleansed the forest, He gives His strength blessing His children with peace. It is His voice that shows us when we are building our own forest from our own hands. His voice is what tears through us, showing us what does not belong. He opens up our needs.

In Revelation, the voice of God is associated with opening doors. In Revelation 4, the door to heaven was open: The Throne of God in heaven has flashes of lightning, rumblings and peals of thunder. There is the opening of first of seven seals. The opening of the 7th seal is the prayers of the saints, which are the incense on the golden altar before God. Then, the angel takes the censer and fills it with fire from the altar and then hurls it to the earth. Then, comes peals of thunder, rumblings and flashes of lightning and an earthquake.

At the end times, God's temple is opened in heaven followed by more thunder. The Lamb stands on Mount Zion and sings a new song before God. At Armageddon the angel pours out his bowl into the air and declares, "It is done!"

In response, the Saints sound like thunder praising God at the wedding of the Lamb. His bride has made herself ready.

Job 28:25, 37, Psalm 18, 29:3, 77:18,
Revelation 4:5, 6:1, 8:5, 14:1, 16:18.

Grace Flies Down

Then, He flew down. The wings of that
Dove and met me in His gentle mercy.
He scooped me up and fixed the
problem.
He led me to just the right person who
could give me exactly what I need
now. Today,
for tomorrow. It is a rescue.
Once more His grace
pulls me through.
Slip knot. I slip
through
the fingers
of the
trap of the enemy.
I am bound by a tie to my Jesus.
Not from my side, but His. His love knot.

Hop in circles

Where am I when they hurt? There. Why
do they continue limp, broken and maimed?
Don't they know I have brought the first aid kit
and I have been trained? I am a physician. I hold
the highest credentials in the school of the Most High.
When you come to Me hurt, you must bring both legs.
You don't realize, but they both need me to make you
be able to walk. Otherwise you hop in circles.
The right leg and the left. The right way is
God's way of righteousness; the road
to His holiness through hearing
His voice. The left leg is
ours. We provide
the other
side
of the relationship to complete
the body
that
will
walk in
victory to bring
healing. Obedience to My
voice is the other leg. That one is yours.

Confirmation of the Word

Sometimes God puts us in a position where others are
looking to us for approval. We don't intentionally go
there, we just end up. Others know that we
are in tune with the Holy Spirit and come to
us for confirmation of messages that they
'hope'
are from God, but are afraid to believe.
It is OK to ask God for messages for them.
He is always happy to confirm His word to
them. Especially, if it is something that He has
put on their heart and He is waiting for them to move
toward the vision.
It is a
good
thing to
encourage
God's people
to listen to His voice and
believe His message for themselves.

Hi jacked Word

Dream:

If I don't understand, sometimes I hold up the dream with a pock-et knife. I threaten it myself, to kill it. I hijack my own airliner to try to bring it down to where I think it should go. My destination.

We are hijacking the words of God; the direction for our lives mid-stream and threatening total destruction of all the passages end up at the wrong destination. We have used the false tutor-like scriptures or words of direction.

We all have been given a ticket, one of our own direction. We've landed on a runway too short, not meant to be where we've gone. But it was hard. There was fog and bad weather. So, we turned on our own GPS. But, we couldn't see out the window. We've spent too much time reflecting on our own thoughts, like looking at our-selves in the mirror. We only notice how imperfect we are.

So, we pass out our little mirrors to the whole planeload of pay-ing passengers all going our direction. They start looking at their own image of who God is and what He wants them to do. All the while, they have been hijacked by our own ideas. But, we held the knife, the words to their throat.

We have embezzled people like money. We've skimmed for our-selves the profit. We have stolen from God what was rightfully His. He wants to grow His people, His way, in His time. We need to dis-embark and unload, abandon our own program. But in our mind it is huge. 707 full of people.

But, our program is doomed to run out of gas because we never calculated and factored in if we have enough to get there because we were not part of the original planning session. The gas in the plane may not equal the trip because now we have taken it to a place it was not meant to go.

We have hi-jacked it to going our own way. It's that five finger thing: We need to put our hands in our pockets and learn to be quiet before God. Less work and more listen. We forget the other side of the I when we trail out on our own vision. He lives to pro-vide us with one. It's the US vision. You, me, and Him. US. The son is the GPS, ATV reflecting His glory because we receive His signal and send it back. We've become a reliable relay.

Like a glass insulator along a wire, we take what He gives and send it down the line. We are not to change what He gives, just to send it down the line. It's the electric fence. The power contained and maintained by Him for a specific purpose. Maintain the Wall; the fence.

His walls of our thinking. Our walls have turned the power off. We thought the electric fence was unsafe, out of control, unreliable, unpredictable, out of date, and not what we need for now. But we are wrong. The insulators are beautiful relays. They are blue glass, and they are perfect for what He needs.

Idiopathic Telepathic

An idiopathic telepathic claims
to know information about someone
she doesn't know. Where did she
get it from? She didn't. That's why
she an idiopathic telepathic.

Other's Sinfulness

Every once in a while, the Holy Spirit
Will tell you of someone who is not
walking in His light upright. He will
tell you of their sin. It is not that
He wants you to run to tell the
other person so that he will
straighten up. No. It is
that God wants
to help you
avoid
the
same
pitfalls
that the
other person is
experiencing and to pray for him.
Parquet
Squares in the entryway. Diverse grains.
Unified diversity at the entrance to a house.
We walk on them when we should walk in them..

The Progression of Hearing the Voice of God

If we want to become sensitive to the voice of God, there are steps that we can take to get us there. It is like a yellow brick road that leads to the Kingdom of God.

We must empty ourselves of the things that keep us from hearing Him. If we are always watching television or talking on the telephone with our friends, then we have no spare time for God. We need to ask Him to weed out our wrong thoughts about who He is and what He intends to do in our lives and the lives of those around us.

Next, we need to seek Him. His Word says that we will find Him when we seek Him with our whole heart. There needs to be a desire for Him within us. We can pray that desire in. I did.

Pray that He gives you a hunger to know Him. Then, pause and listen. Take time out of the schedule to be with Him apart from others. Find a place to be alone with Him and take a piece of paper with to copy down what He says. Ask Him questions and wait for the answer. You will be surprised to see that He talks back. Often, we are in a hurry and do not ask Him the questions. Or, we have already made up our mind what the answer is, so we do not feel the need to seek Him.

When we hear what He wants us to do, then we need to walk that direction. We need to walk into the thinking that He wants to give us. The further we walk into the area of His thinking, and away from the way the world thinks, then we are moving into the anointing that He desires for us.

He will train us Himself, if we take notes when we hear His voice. He will send us to the Scriptures and to individuals that will help us to understand Him more.

Next, comes the discipline. If He gives a dream, do we write it down? If we ask a question, are we prepared with a paper to take note of the answer. If He gives a directive, do we follow it? He wants us to be disciplined children. We are disciplined into obedience.

The more disciplined we become to hearing His voice and walking in the direction of it, the more intricate the instructions can be given to us and we will be trusted to follow them. Just like our children. We can give them more specific directions if we know that they will listen and do exactly what we say. I can trust my daughter to go to the store for me and shop because she writes down everything I say. I do not trust my husband, for example, because he won't make a list and assumes he will remember when he gets there. But, of course, he doesn't and comes home with things that are different from what I need. The same is true with God's instructions for us. He will be more specific if we are more attentive.

We are more useful to minister to others, for instance, if He can tell us to go across the room and deliver a message to someone we don't know. If we are disciplined and in tune, we will hear His voice, then do it. We will be blessed, and the other person will, as well.

After we have become in tune to hearing His voice and disciplined to follow the instructions, then the testing will come. He will give messages that sound weird just to check to see if we will obey. Once, I found myself on a bench alongside a skate park in the middle of the city. I had been practicing an old hymn to sing for a formal group. But, here on the park bench, He told me to sing to the kids. I wasn't sure how they would take it. I was very intimidated by singing out loud. I had my underground CD player, so I could hear the music, but no one else could. They would not hear the music, but would only hear my voice. I laugh, now, when I think what I did. I started singing quietly to myself at about a distance of 100 yards from the skate park. Then, I inched closer and closer. I watched attentively to see if they would all charge me, beat me, and tell me to shut up. I was surprised to see that it didn't happen. Still, I was on the alert to them, thinking that at any moment they would shut me down.

You have to realize that the skate bowl was full of kids with tattoos and skateboards and bikes. I had never visited this place before. After about 20 minutes, I inched my way to a bench. I remember flipping on the music and singing quietly, at first, then louder. Nothing happened. I had safely made it to where God had told me to go. So, I sat there and sang. I sang and sang. And after a while, one by one, the kids came to me to hear. For, I didn't realize that they couldn't even hear my singing over the noise of their skating. But, when they saw my passion for doing it, they recognized it. For, they, too, were attempting to be good at something. They had been practicing to skate, learning precise jumps and twirls. They recognized that I was scared, like them, and that I, too, had come to practice.

So, after a while, they each stopped by to hear the song. And, they encouraged me. It was a test of obedience for me. but, it became so much more. Because they were encouraged, as well, to learn that they could be of encouragement to me.

The song I sang was Great is Your Faithfulness, and I was practicing it to sing for the first time in public, for, God had asked me to sing it at a Christian Writer's Conference karaoke time. And, by practicing with the kids, I learned that I if I could be accepted by them, then I would probably be accepted by the group that I was to sing before.

When we are faithful to believe the word that He has given, then He will reward us. I asked God once why He tests me. If He knows the answer, why does He test me? His response was, "How do you know when the students are ready for the next class if they are not given a test?"

So, the test enables us to move up to the next level, just like in college. We have to pass before going on to the next.

Prayer:
Father, help us to be empty, seeking You whole heartedly and listening when You speak. We ask for Your faithfulness to lead us into the anointing You have for us, train us up in the way we should go, and discipline us gently. Please give us a spirit of instant obedience and the grace needed to pass the tests that You send to us. Amen.

Gold Dust

Salvation wasn't our idea. Why do we build
on our own ideas now? We defile what is pure
with our own dust because we are made of dust.
God has provided us with access to His Wisdom,
Knowledge, Understanding, and Revelation.
He has given us the keys to the Kingdom.
He gives us gold dust that can be
made into whatever He
chooses. His
ideas
are
eternal and priceless.
When,
we
follow
His plan for His ideas,
we build into His desire.

Revelation and Insight

Revelation and insight. What is the difference? Insight
gives us understanding to the ways of God and
revelation takes us to the goal. Insight sets the
mark on the pole vault, and revelation helps
us get over the bar. Revelation shows us
where to grab the pole, where to take
hold of the words of God; where to
claim the promises; the exact spot
needed to get over the bar. Insight
tells us about
the bar. We need discipline coupled to
insight and revelation. That is how the
Bible goes. Shorthand story. God teaches,
sends Jesus, who shows a disciplined life and
teaches it to the disciples who write down the
insight He taught them. Seems to me the last
book in the Bible is Revelation. A good
goal. I don't really like discipline, but I
like where it goes. All discipline
seems hard at the time, but
after a while it bears
the fruit to
eternal life.
Our discipline
comes with grace.
Only
by the blood of the lamb!
And, excuse me if I am wrong,
But isn't that where the Bible ends?
The wedding feast and the supper of the Lamb?

Pacer

Dream:
Turn up the pacer to make artificial blood pressure.
It builds endurance.

Interpretation:
A pacer regulates the heart rate: the rate of the beat of the heart. When we turn up the pacer, it stimulates the heart to beat faster. When the pump beats faster, it puts out more flow. The more flow, the higher the blood pressure. Increasing the rate increases the pressure. When we exercise, our heart rate is increased because the body needs a higher oxygen flow for the muscles to move more.

God wants to be our pacer. He wants to be the one who regulates the flow of our lives. If He is our pacer car, then we can run the race following after Him. When we use His heartbeat, He will set the pace for us. It will be His pace, not ours.

Away from the Flow

The further you are from the flow of the river,
the further you are from that which gives life to the
body of Christ.

Tim, tam,
tamarack, tarmac.
Toad stool, over school,
in a spool. Not done yet
there's more to get.
No time debt, no less lent.
Tim, tam, tamarack,
tarmac.

Tambourines

Tambourines play a tone. Not a tune, but a tone.
Prompted by a rhythm, lead by a tune. Sang a
song, prompted by a heart, instilled by a Spirit.
The tambourines play a tone. They give their
voice, play their part, do their job. Together
with the rest, they help bring about the
culmination of the song.
They provide the finishing
touches. Sometimes, God calls us,
not to be a leader, but to be a follower.
Are we less? No.
We are the
one who
helps to
bring about the climax
of the culmination of unity as the
sweet symphony of
the body of Jesus dances. Powerful miracles

Finished

Finished, done, completed, ended. It happened on
the cross. Why do we act like we're still at war?
Jesus' word stands true. It is finished. And
God doesn't lie. Everything God says is
always true because He is the inventor
of truth. So what happened? We've
been duped, tricked, lured to follow
an idea that is not His. To fight His
battles, God doesn't send Himself.
He sends His power. It flows
through angels, through us and
through His
Word.
The
trickery of the enemy is to
convince us that God's Word
does not have the power it does.
He tries to sell a weak God.
Where's that power again?
The Word, Jesus Christ
sent to us in human
form.
He
embodied the power of God.
What
about
now?
The Holy Spirit
embodies the power of God.
It's not a physical manifestation,
but a spiritual one. That's why He is called a Spirit.
He is that Word today. Same God. Same Jesus. Same power.

Flow of Prophecy

Prophecy flows from the river as it moves.
It doesn't come apart from the river.

Interpretation:
Prophecy is hearing the voice of God. The river is the Holy Spirit. There is no prophecy from God apart from the interpretation by the Holy Spirit. Prophecy cannot be separated from Him. Apart from the Holy Spirit, it is not prophecy from God.

It flows just as a river flows from the source. It moves. Prophecy moves and flows. What was true yesterday may be history today. It is time urgent. There's an expiration stamp to the packages of prophecy that God gives us. Prophetic statements from God are like Christmas pieces of bread that are sent through the mail. They need to be received by a specific date, opened and consumed before they expire.

Sometimes, God will give us messages that are words to tell us what to do for a specific time. If we take the time to interpret these messages on time, then we will know what to do when we get to that specific situation. These are time urgent messages.

That is why it is essential to look at your dreams each night. There may be a message given to you or someone you will come into contact with imbedded within the dream. Over and over, God has given me dreams one day, and the predicament that I need to solve, the next. So, I read all of my dreams the next morning, like cramming for a math test, so I will be ready in case there is a pop quiz.

Paddy Cake

Paddy cake, Daddy cake
God can, plan our hand. His plan,
Bake the cake, to be served by others.

Big Cakes

All the cakes that are baked that call us
to remembrance
 in unity are because of You, Dear Lord.
You are the one that started that.
Calling us to a bigger vision.
I am building a better building.

Tours

Come to Me for the keys.
If you want to give them a tour of the
facility before hand, just go ahead.

The Mansion

I Am. I extend to the length of the chain. Follow
the connections to Me. For in Me is life. The life
is the light of men. Turn on the light. When people
turn on My love light, they see life in a whole new
light. My light. Darkness is dispelled because My
light comes in. It's the truth about the Kingdom
and who's who.
I want all to know who I Am, and who they are.
They need to understand and be given an option
to choose. If they never see who they can be, who
they are meant to be, then the devil wins. Nobody
ever reveals the place I have set aside for them.
These are the mansions I was talking about.
A mansion is a huge place. It is an estate
tended by a governor, a gardener,
a chief, a butler, a driver, and
somebody who waits on you all
the time. My ministry of service starts
by My serving you in a special way. I move you
into the place where I need you to be for My
Kingdom. You will love it. It is a mansion:
A free lifestyle for the rich and famous
sons and daughters of a king.
Then, you allow Me to
serve you in many
capacities as I
meet
your
needs,
it frees you
up to live the life
you were meant to live.
You are hampered by our own pride.
It keeps you back from saying thank you,
accepting His gifts, and living that life of luxury..

Manna

In a demonstration of the power of God coming to His people, Jesus lives to indwell. Power and might are in His hand and His desire is for His children: to share Himself with them in a personal way. He wants to expose His heart to them. But, they push Him aside. They are scared of intimacy.

They are wrong. They think this is Fear of the Lord. It hurts His soul. For as He reaches out to touch them, they draw away. They cringe at His hand when it is extended. Like a wounded lover, He has been repealed by the only one He ever loved. We don't realize we are repealing His desire for us.

Flabbergasted and despondent, He waits for us to soften our heart and open our eyes to realize it is Him. He has sent His gifts. And over and over we have disregarded them and we have thrown them away. We have saved the candy and thrown away the box. It's the box that we need to use to hold more that He would send. The box is the vehicle of our display of the gifts if the Holy Spirit.

For when we refuse to open the gift, we have thrown away the only thing that He has given us to hold the candy that He would put in it to share with others. We took the sweetness ourselves. We came to Him. He met us and shared with us. Then we left.

But you feed your mind with trash; waste, you take what others have thrown aside, and like dogs at the garbage dump you consume the waste from people instead of coming to My table and eating fresh food daily. You are feeding on the ideas of men, rather than Me. They are temporal and do nothing but waste your time, keeping you from the things that are truly important. They keep you in and your children in bondage to sin by placating it, rather than teaching you how to be pure.

We go into the wilderness, but, the manna comes down and we never bring any home to share. For, it has to be put into something.

I have chosen clay vessels to store My manna from heaven in, like the container that held the manna that was placed in the Ark of the Covenant. Through My vehicle with the people I want to share you. Be found in Me.

I will give you fresh bread from heaven every day. I will fill your container to overflowing. The manna comes from heaven. You must gather it. For, you are the container that holds My word.

You see and others eat from the container. They don't eat you. They eat from your hand, what I send. My bread is sent to you. Gather it up and I share it with others to show them how much I love them. You share, not to feed, but to make them hungry to want more and come to seek Me in the desert on their own. Wilderness.

That's my idea of wilderness. Learn to be needy; to live on what I send day by day. Be hungry for My word, none else. Put away all other food and seek My heavenly food; My manna from heaven.

Come, be found in Christ. He is your eternal righteousness. He covers it all. Be endowed with Him. Claim what He holds in His hand. Endowment as a dowry.

Bakery

Dream:

I brought my mother to a bakery. It was a huge building the size of a hanger. We walked by the place where they have special rolls. They bake them for seasons. Now they were making things for Easter and Spring. I picked up one and handed it to her. Then, I show her all of the loaves of bread. It smells wonderful. There are all kinds of loaves of bread on long tables. The special seasonal breads come out on conveyor belts, and they are wrapped up by the women.

Interpretation:

My mother is my trainer; mother Wisdom. We go together to the place where the bread comes out directly from the baker. Jesus is the bread. He is the Word given to us. God has bread waiting for us. It is already baked for us and ready to eat. But, there are also some loaves of bread coming out on a conveyer belt.

I think of dreams as loaves of bread. Sometimes, we are given a long detailed dream. It is like a loaf of bread that needs to be sliced or broken off to be consumed. Then, there are other times when we are given little dreams, or clips, like seasonal breads that can be popped into our mouth easily.

All that God wants to teach is like bread to us. We need to eat and digest it to be able to flow out of us.

When He shows all that He wants to feed us, then we must reach out our hand to take it. He puts it in front of us in a place where it is easy to get. We go to the place where He hangs out, to His hanger and hang out with Him. The bread of Jesus' Word is found in the hanger, the place of communion with God. (You know, like an airplane?)

Bread is a staff of life and can be used for a lot of things, just as God's teaching to us can be used for many things. There are several varieties of bread. This dream demonstrates to us that God can use similar ingredients to come up with very different foods that are all the staff of life.

When we have a dream, it is like an uncut loaf of bread. We need to take the knife, the Sword, the Scriptures, to it to figure it out. The scriptures will 'cut' the bread so we can consume it. As the Holy Spirit speaks through the Scriptures, He will help to cut through into our sub-consciousness to make us to understand the true meaning of the dream that God is trying to convey to us. He doesn't slice the bread for us, He gives us the knife. When we put 'the loaf' up to the Scriptures, then we will be given insight to the meaning. The Old Word cuts the new word to prepare it so it can be edible.

We can serve it to others as well, when we break off a piece of our loaf. To do this, we must combine ourselves with it. We give some of our own experiences with it. We tell them of the teaching that God has given us, and how we applied it. This is bread that we have broken, because God has broken us apart. He has separated our soul from our flesh and our spirit. He has shown us more of Himself and His love for us. Testimony combines with the Word.

But, the dream shows another kind of bread. It is the 'seasonal breads' that are coming off of the conveyer belt directly from the kitchen. They come from the direct line where they are baked by the baker, God himself. They come already in bite-sized pieces of bread. They can be eaten in a few chews by almost anyone. These are like the 'word poetry that I have sprinkled throughout this book. They are the 'seasonal' breads that do not need interpretation because they are simple and timely.

Bread of Presence

When we stay in the presence of God; when we don't leave His hanger, then we will immediately share the bread with the one who raises us.

We will take it back to our upbringing; the teaching that we have been trained on, our Mother, present it to that body of knowledge and let her take the first bites. It is like giving an offering back to God. When He gives us a 'word', we should give it back to Him; reflect it back in His presence before we speak it out. It is like saying, 'What else do you want me to add with this, God?"

We give Him another opportunity to clarify Himself during a time when we are listening to Him and attentive to His voice free from distractions. Perhaps the first word was given during a time when we were asleep, as in a dream, or during a time when we weren't really sure that we were paying attention. We should promptly take it back to Him and ask Him what to do with it. He will tell us. Have paper ready to copy His additional words.

When God is allowed to clarify Himself, He always talks. He has shown me that when I open a drawer, there are drawers within it. He has been waiting for us to listen. Then, we are showing our gratitude to Him for the Word. It is like saying 'grace' before we eat. Before we 'serve' others with the Rhema word that He gives us, we need to thank Him for it.

We should say, "Thank You, God. Do you have anything else to add to your word before I share it?"

Many times, when we bring the word back to Him, He will expand it and make it to fit a broader audience. A word that we thought maybe for only a small group, now, becomes applicable to a much larger group. God loves to expand His voice. We need to let Him. Our mouth can become the speaker to others who are not paying attention to make them hungry to hear His voice.

The anointing will teach us. He has given us the Holy Spirit as our interpreter. He has also given us Spiritual Gifts. He matures these gifts, He will use them as tools to teach us. When we have a dream and interpret it, then He uses both to teach us. The Holy Spirit working through the anointing is what teaches us. That's when we build a sandwich.

God's Oreo Sandwich

I think that if there was a chocolate
bar called understanding, it would be
cream filling sandwiched between
two cookies. For, God puts
us in the palm of His hand.
He threads His fingers
between ours and
pulls us close to
Himself.
Then,
He
covers
us
with
His other.
Father, please fill
us with understanding
of Your love. Thread Your
fingers through ours and pull us in.

Troublemakers and Dogs

The dream:

   As I am going up the stairs to my father's house, I look through
the window and see dogs in the basement. I drop white (poop) duty.
I let it go, and it falls on the white rug. The dogs see me come, and
they come and try to eat it. I wrestle the dogs and throw the poop
out the door with a kitten.

Interpretation:

As we walk on the path toward where we are supposed to be,
we will encounter those who will cause us problems. Our Father
knows they are there and is telling us to beware of them. We can
look through the window that He has provided for us and see them
coming. The window is the place where we see Him. We understand the reflection of His voice as He speaks into our spirit with
messages that cannot be heard by the enemies.

He reminds us, in this dream, that each time we release something
from the Kingdom of God that we are instructed to do, the enemy
will be there quickly to try to destroy it. Dogs will eat anything.
That is the picture we are to get.

Dogs are, many times, stupid. I know I have had a dog that I took
for a walk on the beach once. It was supposed to be a nice romantic
walk with my husband on the sand. We took the dog along, thinking that He would like to get out. The walk turned into a nightmare.
We couldn't keep him out of the water. He wanted to swim. Of
course, all of the sand caked in his fur in the wet spots. If that was
not enough, He managed to find a dead seagull to haul around and
roll in. What we brought back to our hotel was a mangy, smelly
dog covered with clumps of sandy mud.

God would remind us that the spiritual battles with the enemy are
not a game. He is out to destroy us, and Satan has an army of dogs.
These dogs will try to tear up everything we do.

   They don't eat it because it contains the Word of God, and they
cannot endure that, but they will try to rent it so that it is no good
to anyone else. It is like chewing up a term paper. They don't eat

it, they just destroy it, so others can't read it.

In the dream, I take what has come from me (funny picture of white poop) and throw it out the door. I toss it out the door that God provides for me. He will empower His Word to fulfill His mission. When He gives a vision and promises, He will see it through to the end.

In the dream, I toss it out the door with a kitten. A kitten is symbolic of a pet that is warm, soft, and cuddly. God wants us to send His messages out with His warm heart. They should be sent out with gentleness and compassion like one would hold a kitten. He reminds us that the messages are for His children. We need to give them to the kids like we would provide them with a kitten.

Scripture Study: Troublemakers

There will be those within the Church who refuse to follow the directions that God gives them into their lives. They refuse to listen to their visions, their heart, and their dreams. They refuse to base their ministry on the voice God directed by His love. It is not our job to expose the foundations of others but to realize that any structure that is not built on the love of God will fail. We are wasting our time with them. Where there are dogs, there is dissension, discouragement, doubt, and anger within the Church.

These trouble makers will not support us that seek to listen to God for His blueprints. Some will say that our progression is too slow. They are not in tune with God's timing, but their own. They will see our potential with their eyes instead of the eyes of God. They will say that we are rebellious to leadership because we won't join the pack. Instead, they say, we want to go off on our own listening to God for ourselves. They will cause us to doubt God and His work in our lives. They will try to tear down what God is building. They will accuse us of causing dissension by listening to God on our own, seeking selfish ambition, which leads to jealousy.

Dogs: False Prophets

There are also dogs in the Kingdom of Satan. God wants us to be aware of them. They are false prophets.

There are true prophets and there are false prophets. God wants us to be aware of the characteristics of these 'dogs' and to know what to do with them.

There are those among us in the Church who look like prophets but are not. They are like dogs that carry off the words of God and tear it up rather than giving a true prophecy that feeds the Children of God.

We can tell what their intentions are by what they do within the Church body. They are not caring individuals. They do not allow themselves to be available to the needs of the Children. They don't notice who needs an encouraging word. They can't tell if someone is sick in the body or spirit unless they are told because their spirits are not in tune with the flock.

They rarely pray and fast for anyone except themselves. Instead, they are insensitive and hurt feelings of those they are supposed to be patching up. This causes a church to be torn apart, not brought together.

They care only for their own relationship with God. They put everyone else second. They come into God's presence, but won't share it. They have one prayer for when they are alone with God and another for when they are with others. They don't open themselves up to others to share how the love of Christ has changed them personally. They push people away from God because they refuse to reflect the true character of God. They will not show others their weaknesses. They protect their identities, and in doing this, they do not disclose God's identity. They are private people.

Their ministry is not built on a relationship with God through the love of Christ. Because the love of God is the only stable foundation, their ministry is unstable. They compensate with faith in themselves that they have heard the 'call' of God on their lives and their ministry.

They become bold and arrogant using their own logic rather than the Holy Spirit to direct their speech.

Consequently, they attract others who use the same logic to direct their lives. The problem is that the foundation of this logic is from our sinful nature; our mind, not the Wisdom of God.

These individuals attract young Christians, who have not learned to draw from the wisdom of God and are still relying on their minds to direct them. Therefore, they propagate errors in young believers. Because their goals for their own ministry make sense to themselves, they reject teaching from the Holy Spirit and His authority within their education.

They feel the need to justify their thinking, so they begin to speak abusively toward whatever they don't understand. They reject heavenly representations of God because they don't make sense to their fleshly mind. They follow things that they can understand with the five senses; the here and now.

They do not give God credit for the miracles that He is performing, even when they are done in front of them, because they do not make sense to them.

They feed off of themselves. They feed themselves with the attention that others pay to them; how important they are to the ministry. They feed off of their 'position' within the church. They know that they are good at making decisions because they are sure that they are 'hearing from God'. Actually, they hear their own minds talk to themselves. Their own voice has become their food.

Then, when they use it as food for others, it has no eternal value and causes famine within the Church. They follow their instincts; they are urging instead of the urging of the Holy Spirit.

These individuals find fault with others. They have a beam in their eye, so that is what they see in others. The eye needs to be clear to see the sin of others, or else all we see is our own sin reflected in them. It is like looking out a window at night. Our eye is the window. If we look out the window and we are dark inside, then we will only see the reflection of ourselves, not the other person. They need others to tell them how great they are, so they help them along, giving them the words to write. They flatter others, then expect the same in return.

When confronted with a Dog

The true prophets of God will come against false prophets. God will allow people to turn to true prophets. Often they are alone because the word that God has given is unpopular. The true prophets will be slandered by the false prophets, the dogs.

It is a confrontation of the Wisdom of God verses the wisdom of men. They will mock and insult the teaching of God as senseless and silly. They will encircle us to tear apart what God has given us. They lay wait for us to conspire against us. They snarl like dogs and prowl. They put confidence in their flesh and their own wisdom.

We cannot fight them with our own strength, because they outnumber us. If we fight in their arena, they will win flesh against flesh. We cannot win the 'mind' battle and make the word of God make sense to them. God will deliver us with the Sword of His Word because it is true. We do not need to defend it, only to speak it.

When we see false prophets, we are to pray for them. As God has shown us mercy when we have doubted, we are to show them the same mercy. We are to ask God to bring down the false teaching and their nets that entrap. We should pray that their own pride is their downfall; that the curses and lies that they utter will come back to them.

When we find those false prophets that will listen to us we are supposed to teach them about relying on the Wisdom of God and His love, rather than their own minds to interpret God's Word. To be able to minister to them, we need to get very close to being able to help them. It will arouse fear in us, because we will be afraid that we may be sucked into their logic, but if we pray for God to give us a vision of purity, then He will unravel for both of us the matrix built by Satan. He will be faithful to show the line where the flesh and the spirit meet and differentiate between them for us.

Psalms 22.16, 59, Jeremiah 15.3, Ezekiel 34, Matthew 7.6, Philippians 3.2, Peter, Jude, Revelation 22.15

Stay on the Trail

Thwart a temptation, avert a hazard.
Be brave, be bold.
Be one to believe that the trail
you walk on has been put there
for you.
Avoid crossing over to the other trails.
It's a hazard.
For, when you go off the trail
there could be wild animals,
poison oak and the unknown dangers.
Without direction from the Holy Spirit,
we are like a boat adrift without a motor.

Lemon Aid

Children sell lemon aid for prophet.
They give nothing, but get everything.
They are just like those who sell to others words not from God.
Those children have mixed the recipe and stand at the corner
calling out to those who don't need their aid, but buy it
anyway because they are thirsty.
That's why we call them children. So are we.

Hiding with the Dog Food

Dream:

There was a family. Somehow they end up living in a place that others thought was abandoned. It is a hiding place. But, they live secretly. Daily, they sweep the remains of their presence into a pile. No one notices it getting larger.

One day when the owner of the house came back suddenly, the daughter swept the pile the other direction. It was dog food swept next to fractured pottery chunks (both brown). It looked the same to her. Then, she hid in the shadows. But, when the man came, He noticed that there was dog food there. Then, He saw her feet below the shadows. He found the people hiding.

Interpretation:

There is a growing presence of abandoned children within the house of God. They are the ones under the table treated like those 'Outside the covenants." There are leftover dog food and broken pottery. These are evidence of things left for the dogs. The broken pottery indicates something that was built but then shattered. These are things that the dogs are meant to feed on.

There is a growing presence of abandoned children within the Kingdom of God. They are living under the promises of God rather than within them. They have the right to feed at the table with the children but are hiding like dogs. They are feeding off of broken dreams, fractured lives, and scraps rather than the true word of God. They don't want the dog food and keep sweeping it but don't have any place to dump it. There is no trash can. They are fed food meant for the dogs.

Jesus has returned. The abandoned children have been noticed because He saw the pile of scraps and broken dreams left to her. Children have it all mixed up. We have confused broken dreams with food meant for animals. We are afraid to be revealed because we have been living off of the dog food and don't want anyone to find out.

We have been hiding in the shadows, afraid of being found out. We would rather hide from what God wants to tell us than have real food meant for the Children. We are afraid of the true word of God in our lives. Will He come with rebuke? What will He say? Are we afraid of God? What kind of image of Him do we have?

God is saying that our feet are sticking out under the curtains. He sees them. He knows that we are hiding, living off the scraps of the word that have been given to others. We are not hiding our brokenness from him. We have been content to live amongst our depravity.

The Father wants to come out at night when we hide. He wants to come into our dreams. Do we hide from Him and live off the dog food, or are we going to open up and listen to His word to us?

Psalms 139, Isaiah 45.9, 64.8, Matthew 15.26-27

Discipline for Others

When we see God's Children being bad,
remember, they are His Children.
They are His responsibility, not ours.
He will discipline His Children. Remember, He did you?

At-A-Boy Motivation

At-a-man has a pallet of tricks. It motivates with at-a-boys.
These ministries mimic high school clubs. They bribe us into
service with pats on the back, telling us how good we are. The
game goes something like this: You pat my ego, and I will pat
yours. I will tell you how great your speech is, and you tell me
how great mine is. I will push to sell your tapes from the
pulpit, but when you speak, you make sure to ask them
to put money in the plate. I'll encourage people to
come to your concert, while you send them to
prayer group. Give the people that faithfully
show up for service special name tags, so
others can know who they are. After all,
they have contributed so much to the
Church. Then, we will both make a
pact to support one another and
tell how great our ministries are.
That way, neither can be guilty
of building themselves up.
For, they have made a
pact to build
each
other
up.
It sounds like they are
supporting their Christian brethren, but
in reality, they are feeding their own ministry,
for they expect the other person to send people and
money their direction. They send people to one another by
patting each other on the back. This regimen has a pallet of
games. All colorful ways to trick us into joining their team.

Prophetic Prayer

If wishes were bushes, the roadsides along our freeway would be constantly in bloom. Because what we plant always grows when we concentrate on it. We spend more time decorating the roadside than paving it. Why wish when we can have? Pray.

Window of Opportunity for Salvation

The Dream:
He got sick and died. He was my brother in law. I dream that he lives. He starts to move and we watch. Then he comes back to life and is grabbing at me, chasing me around. He is sick and has a green puddle coming out from his body. There is a surgeon there who says he needs to have his gall bladder removed. It's obvious that it's needed because he looks so sick. The surgeon tells him that he needs the surgery, then, he must die; He must go back to being dead. The brother in law cries and does not want to stay dead.

A woman is standing in front of his face, but she freezes, unable to talk. I know her. She is someone who has come to me recently, saying that she has been praying for God to send her someone to help her grow closer to God. The television is loud, and there are many people in that place. It is very noisy. I scream over the noise to tell him how to be saved.

To me, it is simple to lead a man to Christ. But, others have never done it. All I did was ask God, "Why would You bring a man back to life, to have him die again?"

And, God responded, "There is only one reason why I would give him this window of opportunity. For, to us, the dead guy is still dead, even though he does not feel the same way. Surgery, at this point, is therapeutic, not meant to heal him. He is dead. We consider him dead."

Then, I realize it is a spiritual condition, not a physical one. The reason had to be for his salvation. He looked dead to me, even though he is talking and following me around. Because, the truth is that, until he is made alive spiritually, he remains dead. We don't think it is that bad being dead, because we are alive, but, he seems to.

Interpretation:

There are those who follow the law rather than the love of God. The law isn't meant to save, it merely shows us our sin, so that we will see our need to be saved. Those who know about God's rules, yet never come to know Him personally, are dead, even while they walk. They are sick, in need of a physician, yet they do not seek one because they do not think they need one. It is much easier to convince a poor convict that he needs Jesus than a successful Church going, individual. The poor convict knows that he is a sinner in need of a Savior, but the other man may not be so keenly aware of his need.

Some are near us that are really dead, even though we think they are alive. We do not know one another's heart. Those who are not alive through Salvation in Jesus are like walking dead people. Their spirit is dead, but their body is alive. They die twice because there is physical death and a spiritual death.

In my dream, the brother in law is alive, and he starts to move. I envision life for him, and it begins to happen. As I pray for him, the gift of life is extended to him. He is grabbing at me because he knows that I have something to offer. I know how to provide him with what he needs to live eternally.

He needs his gall bladder out. The gall bladder makes it so that we can absorb fats into our system. The Holy Spirit is oil. This man needs the oil of the Holy Spirit to be absorbed into his system. He cannot absorb it. He was never saved, so he was unable to absorb the things of God.

We cannot have the Holy Spirit without salvation through the blood of Jesus. The surgeon will remove the capacity for him to know the Holy Spirit. Then, at that point, he will truly be dead.

The man cries out for help, but others are very busy with their own schedules. They are distracted watching television. I pray because I see a vision, just like television. Instead of allowing the world to give me their visions, I rely on God to provide me with His. And, God's vision for this man is to save him from eternal damnation. A problem with this man getting saved is that the woman who is put in front of him doesn't know what to do. Why doesn't she know what to say?

What is obvious to me is only obvious because I ask God for the answer. But, when I ask Him, He makes it plain to me what the problem is. I believe the window of opportunity is for the woman as much as the man. God has given her an opportunity to be used within His kingdom, yet she does not know how to use the key to open the door of opportunity He has put before her. It takes more than just being available, to be ready to respond when God asks us to. We need to study the Bible and learn what it says.

Then, we need to learn how to ask God questions and wait for His responses. As He gives the responses, we need to be willing to follow His leading. It was noisy in the environment that He placed me in, and, yet, I heard His voice because He dropped the message into my spirit through my heart because it was open to receive the answer. I waited for the answer before I responded to the man. In the dream, he chases me around for a while. I don't get involved until I know what to do. The man had a dead spirit that could only be made alive through regeneration by the invitation of the Holy Spirit into his life.

If you know within your heart that you are dead, and don't want to stay dead, here is a prayer that you can pray to have the assurance that you will live forever:

Father, I know that I am a sinner in need of a Salvation. I don't want to have my gall bladder out, but I want the Holy Spirit to enter into my body. Make my body to become the temple of the Holy Spirit. Please forgive me of my sin through the blood of Jesus Christ and give me eternal life. I renounce Satan and all of the world's ideas. Please teach me to love You... Amen.

211

Do not fear what they fear; do not be frightened. But in your hearts set apart Christ as Lord. Always be ready to give an answer for the hope that you have. But do this with gentleness and respect.
Romans 5-8, I Peter 3.15

Eternal Purpose

He was.
He is. We are.
Let's push forward together.
God is eternal.
His plans have been for us since eternity past.
We have become His children with an eternal purpose.
He lives within us to achieve that purpose
through us.

Reflection Pool

You walk around until you find the reflection of your prayers. Then, you go stand under them. They are the start of something great.

Become In Us

Overcome our badness with Your goodness. Become in us,
Yourself, we pray, O Lord. Father, Son, and Holy Spirit,
Three in One.
Is He three gods in one God. No. Three ways to show
us the same God who is one personal being. He shows
us His different parts so we can relate to Him. Jesus
became the man; the flesh, the physical part of God.
He was born as a child on earth to Mother Mary,
yet He always existed.
For, time isn't the same to Him as it is to us.
We have limits to time as we live in our world.
He doesn't. The Holy Spirit speaks to our soul.
Through His voice we hear God. Through
Him we are enabled to become obedient
to holiness. With these two, we have the
voice of God and the manifestation
of Him. Why do we need the
Father? Who is He?
Creator
and
deliverer of my soul. O caring
One who nurtures us as children,
leads
us as a Shepherd,
tends us as sheep. He is
the One who gives us direction to pray.
Like a point on a Compass. He provides the heading.

Golden Heart

The Dream:
You bring your healing life through the deliverance of prayer. Prayer is the golden heart of the seeds of the Kingdom of God.

Interpretation:
When we become Children of God through belief in Jesus Christ as our Savior, we become sensitive to inner voice of the Holy Spirit. We receive a spirit of adoption as sons and our spirit is made alive. All of a sudden, we realize that we need a father. We know that we have been orphans until now, and need to be raised by parents. Our spirit, that has been dormant, in a state of decay and death, now is given life through the blood of Jesus. He gives us a transfusion. The spirit starts to become hungry, like a little baby and cries out for attention from its father, God.

We have all been formed with the ability to know God because He put it there when He created us. But, it is not awakened without Him awakening it. When we are given life through Jesus, then this aspect of our personality is given the same type of life that Jesus has. It gives a sense of recognition to understand God stuff.

We are like a canvas that has been unveiled. But, we are blank, however, until we allow God to write on us. The canvass is our heart. It is our mind, our soul. We can write on it ourselves, allow others to write on it, or, we can ask God to etch on our heart what is important to Him.

Many of the things that are important to God, are explained in the Scriptures. He left us a book to tell about Himself. But, in addition, He has also, given us the Holy Spirit who will write on our hearts His messages. If we become faithful to wipe our slate clean on a regular basis, we can be open to receive His messages into our heart. Jesus is the one we go to who will help us to purify our minds and hearts and make them ready for the voice of the Holy Spirit. Then, we need to remove the clutter between our hearts and minds so that the messages will be able to surface. It does no good to receive a message from the Holy Spirit that comes in hieroglyphics when we are unable to make it useful for our lives. It becomes like a dream that we cannot remember. There is no way to respond to words we cannot hear. There are many things that clutter the path between our hearts and minds. Often, we don't even realize what they are.

He has made a provision for this, as well. He continues to make a way for us to hear His voice, clear the path to our heart, interpret the messages, and help us to live them to the full extent of their promise.

And, we have to go to Him for help to hear our heart. For, we don't even know our own heart, unless God tells us. We are the first to deceive ourselves and take the easy road, so we need to ask Him for help. To be sure, He will be faithful to show us anything that is blocking the way.

Then, when God tells us what the problem is, we ask for help. That is deliverance through prayer. It is the seeds to the Kingdom of God. When we pray what He wants, He grows what He plants.

Proverbs 16:18, Hosea 4:12. Rom 8:15,
I Corinthians 2:16, Hebrews 10:16

Our Pond

Green frogs jump in the pond that was given to them.
God has provided us a place where He wants us
to live. As they have a pond, we have one as
well. They hop from rock to rock. We are
not frogs, though. God wants us to go
from rock to rock; revelation to
revelation by walking on water.
If we sit on a certain promise
that He gave us long ago
instead of attempting
to walk into it,
then we will be
like a frog.
We were
not made to sit,
but walk. Not to hop, but flow.
For, He has come and is coming back.
It is there that we move within the provision.
Between His revelation of who He is and
who we are through His provision. Yes,
there are lily white promises
and there is the
padding of grace.
But, we are not meant to
walk grace to grace, but within the
power of the Holy Spirit and provision
of the gifts He has put into our hands. The
miracles of God come from Him
through people. So, we are
frogs that have become princes only
because of our position within the Kingdom as
His children. When we flow, instead of jump, others
will think us to be slow, but they will remember us forever.

Fishing in the Closet

Dream:

A friend of mine is in a walk-in closet sitting in the dark. She has a fishing pole and is fishing in a small well. She has a little stool and is straddling the fishing hole, intently staring into it.

I come into the closet, turning the light on as I go and ask her, "What are you doing?"

She says," I'm a fishin'. There's a fish in there, and I'm gonna catch um."

I look into the ditch. Sure enough, there is a healthy full-grown trout swimming around. The only other thing in the hole is a tin can. She is fishing for all she is worth, very diligently trying to catch this fish with her fishing pole.

Then, it's like her time is up for the day, and she says, "Well, that's it for today, I will be back tomorrow...and I will catch that fish."

She grabs her tackle box and goes out of the closet.

Interpretation:

I have a friend that is praying in her prayer closet. It is a place where she goes for a specific amount of time each day to ask God for certain things that are on her mind. She has specific requests, like fish, that she is hoping to catch. Fish are representative of individuals that need to be converted in the Bible. Jesus tells Peter when He calls him as a disciple that he will no longer catch fish, but men. Peter was a fisherman before Jesus called him to become a disciple. It's not to say that people are fish, but they are like fish, in that they need to be captured, hooked, and brought into the boat. The boat that Jesus provides is one of safety. But, Jesus shows Peter, later on in the Gospels, how to catch fish, His way. He instructs him where to toss the net.

In the same way, my friend is going into her closet, fishing with a rod and reel, rather than a net. If she had a net, then surely she could catch this single fish.

In addition, she is fishing in the dark. If she turned on the light, it would make things easier. Jesus is the light. He gives the light of

217

the knowledge of the direction we are to walk. If she were to ask Him for direction, then it is like she turned on the light.

Many of us think that prayer is done in a 'closet'. We do our praying in the dark without direction from God. We base our prayers on 'fishing' for what God might want for us. We wonder if we 'can' do things; we preserver in our prayer closet without direction from Him.

She comes every day with the same request, the same tackle and the same rod. She has the same things that she is fishing for, looking for the answers to be fulfilled, and seeking the provisions from God. To her, she will be persistent until she catches the fish, for she knows God will be faithful.

But, she is missing a few of the things that will make her prayers answered. I have had a lot of fun with the interpretation of this dream. And, I want to point out that God has given me another dream about this same woman saying that she excels in the many colors of prayer. He has raised her up as an example for us. For, she is an example of persistence, not only knocking on His door but being willing to enter into the dark places of her soul to seek His answers. For Him to say that she excels in the many colors of prayer means that she holds Him to many covenants, like the colors of the rainbow. And, He loves to be held to His promises. She is claiming the promises. Good idea.

Bible Study: Good prayer VS best prayer.

When we ask God what He wants before we pray it, then it is like turning the light on in the closet. It is possible to have God directed prayer. *Take for instance, that I want to meet you at a restaurant. If I get there before you, I can order for you. If I don't ask you what you want, I may not order what you like. Perhaps, if I know you well enough, I can predict what you will eat, but it will not be as good as if you ordered it yourself.*

When we have an opportunity to ask God what He wants for our prayer before we pray it, it is similar to asking Him what He would want us to order for Him from the restaurant. If we ask, then pray what He tells us to, He will do it for sure because we will have prayed 'into' His will. Prayer that is directed by God is the best. It is on target.

'Can Do' Prayer.

Often, when we come to God, we have ideas of what we want Him to do. These prayers are directed by us. We direct the prayer time. The time becomes filled with a barrage of questions without expecting the answer. We think that the answer will be revealed when the circumstances are changed that we are praying for. For example, if we are praying for someone to be healed, we ask for healing, then, look for the answer to be when he is healed. We assume that the answer is in the healing. We claim verses in the Bible on healing, then ask God to be true to His word. *We look to the Bible, rather than Him.* We are forgetting that He is alive.

The first time I gave my Bible away, God's voice came to me in the middle of Church. He said, *"Sheri. Give your Bible to your friend."*

I asked Him, *"Why?"*

He responded, *"Because you love it too much. I am not a book. I am a person."*

I had grown to see the book as Him. It's not.

This is not interactive prayer. It is one sided. It's kind of like an interrogation of God without giving Him time to answer. Here are some examples of 'can dos' that we pray.

Canned Barrage Prayer

Can you hear me, God? Are you there? Do you exist for real? Do you have a hearing problem?

Can You be called on by man? Is it possible to have a relationship with You while I am still on the earth? Am I too little and You too big?

What can You do for me God? Why would this relationship be needed for me? What do You have to offer me outside of what I already have?)

Can You do this? Is it possible?
Can You do this for me? Is it Your will for Me?
Can I have this? Does He want it for Me. Am I worthy?
What Can I do? Is there something I am not doing?

Then, there are the canned prayers:

Canned prayers. Rote printed prayers that don't speak our heart on the issue. They are someone else's heart spoken to God at a specific time in their life, but do not have any meaning for us, today.

Other types of canned prayers. Do we come into His presence the same way all of the time? Do we honestly think He is listening? Would we say the same thing to someone all the time if we thought they were listening?

We think that if we are persistent He will listen. He is like a stubborn old man who will finally give in if we keep on bugging Him. *What is a fervent prayer of a righteous man?*

Prayer Rainbow

When we want an outward display of His covenants toward us, we ask, "God, You love me. Will You show it to me?"

If we claim a few promises, then those colors will show to God. The more promises of His Word we claim, the more colors will be displayed to Him. We don't know, without asking Him, which colors are needed for the fulfillment of the promise to be in acted by Him.

When there is the right mixture of colors, the bow will be displayed. It is external evidence of a covenant relationship between Us. There is always a covenant, but there is not always an outward display of it. We can even continue to pray after the covenant is displayed!

220

And there will be more colors. More display of His power and light!

For example, when I was praying for myself, God told me that He wanted to give me the gift of Wisdom. Well, I know that Proverbs is all about Wisdom, so I began to pray in the book for my life. I think I got about as far as chapter 20. But, I started with the first few chapters. I know God began to bless me with His Wisdom. I could feel it coming out in my speech with others. But, I continued to pray other chapters of the Bible to claim more colors of the covenant.

Problems in prayer

Challenging God

There may be prayers that are not answered because our motivation is wrong. *Do we challenge God to do something?*

One time I was sent to a woman's room where her son was in the ICU on a ventilator. He was in his 20's and had a terrible form of cancer. She asked me to pray with her. She had Bible verses tacked all over the room. The place was cluttered with Bibles and religious stuff. It looked like a shrine. She informed me that God was going to heal her son; that God would prove all the doctors wrong. They had said that her son would die, but she knew that God would not let her son die, but heal him.

She had challenged the doctors, her family and God to heal her son. I took her hand and the hand of her son and did not pray for healing. I prayed for grace to be given to each of them.

I believe that I was the only one who did not pray how she wanted, for in about three weeks, I was called to go to her bedside again. A respiratory therapist came and got me, saying that the mother was asking for me. Now, I had only prayed with her for a few minutes several weeks earlier, but yet she remembered me.

This time was different. They were removing her son from the ventilator to die. His body was spent, his time was up.

I went to the room and found all the Bibles thrown in a corner on the floor. All the family was gone, except the mother. And, she was weeping bitterly over her son. He had just been removed from the ventilator and was gasping for air in his final moments.

I went to his side and took his hand. He was a sturdy black boy. I could tell that he had the potential to play basketball, for he was tall.

But, now that cancer had won. His body was gaunt, and he was pale. Racked with pain and torment, he was seeking rest.

First, I prayed for my own grace from God. Then, I bound up the spirit of agony that permeated the room. God showed me that the enemy had invaded the room with a spirit of agony and was tormenting them. So, I bound and asked for the blood of Jesus to remove the spirit of agony.

Then, I asked the mother if she had a Bible. I knew she did because I remember her flashing it in my face the month earlier. She riffled under some other books and papers that were on the floor and came up with a large red Bible.

I laid it on the bed within reach of her son and told her, "Give him to God. Satan can't take something that you don't own. For, if you still own your son, in your heart, then when he dies, you will become angry at God. Satan will be able to use it against you to tear your relationship from Him and your family. For, if you don't own him, he can't be taken from you. Satan can't take something if we have nothing."

Then, I prayed for them both quietly, in tongues.

After a time, she put her hand on the Bible and prayed to God, giving her son to Him.

Then, I turned to her, my face indented with my own tears, and told her, "Now, lay his hand on the Bible and pray with him to give you to God."

I saw it just as Jesus was on the cross, he released his mother and allowed her to be released into the hand of his friend. I could never have come up with this on my own. I had to ask Him for the answer.

The mother laid the bony hand of her nearly dead son on the Bible, the book she had trusted in, and entrusted him to the person of God, rather than the promise within the book. She realized that she had taken the promises of her own convenience and tried

222

to twist the arm of God by using His Bible. It was wrong. So, she needed to repent and do things His way: Let Him be in charge of the situation, no matter how much it hurt.

She did it, and he did it with his final breaths. He gave his mother to God, and he had a wonderful sense of relief, knowing that God would take care of her.

Then, I said, "Where is your son going now?"

"To heaven," She responded.

"Why don't we help him get there. Do you have any music here in this room?"

I knew she had music because I had heard it coming out of the room during the weeks earlier. So, again, she ruffled under some bags and found a CD player and some Jesus rap music. It was the kind that he used to listen to when he was well.

And, she fired up the CD player. I took them both into my arms and as I cried with them, feeling their pain, I prayed for God's true healing power to flow through their lives and for Him to welcome them into His presence with joy.

As I left that room, I was in awe of God. For, I twenty minutes earlier I had entered a room where Satan was stealing a son from a mother and tearing up a family, leaving a mother angry with the God she had grown to love. But, when I left, the hall was filled with Jesus rap music and a mother singing praises to her Lord for enabling victory to be won.

More problems in prayer

Instability

Maybe our prayers are unstable. Do we pray one way one day and another way the next because we aren't sure what God wants and don't want to be found without the answer being prayed in by us?

One time, was with my brother and another came to him to be prayed for because he was sick. He laid his hand on the person and prayed like this, "Lord, if it be Your will heal this dear brother. If it is not Your will, then help him to endure it."

I was shocked. My mouth stayed open as the person walked away,

I asked my friend, "What was that?"

I continued, "That prayer is not to the God I know. One of God's names is 'healer'. Why didn't you pray for healing?"

His response was, "I'm not sure if God will heal him and I don't want his faith in God to waver, so, I left it up to God. He can heal him if He wants."

I guess this prayer has no risk. But, a prayer that has no direction has none.

Following designs of others

Often, we see our prayer line going into a ditch instead of before the throne room of God. Do we feel it is going down instead of up? Maybe we are following the designs of other men for prayer instead of God sent designs.

Are we drawn to other people, like the prayer group, to pray, or are we drawn to God, first, then, caused to pray? When God is on the other end of the line, He will draw us. We should not be pulled to Him by our needs and requests, but, by our relationship with Him. If we allow God to come to us first, then His will rises up in us and drives our prayers.

The first prayer group I encountered was filled with powerful individuals who spoke loudly. I felt that if I didn't speak loudly, then I must not be praying correctly. I didn't realize that we each pray differently. We cannot pattern our prayer style after others. It is like putting on shoes that don't fit. We won't be able to get far in them before we have to take them off. We may as well start out with our bare feet.

Scheduled Prayer

Is our prayer life turned off and on like a light? Do we go in and out of prayer time? Is our prayer life turned off and on like a light? Do we go in and out of prayer time? God wants to be with us continually. He doesn't just want us to pray at our times of convenience that have been preset. We don't come to Him, but open ourselves to allow Him to come to us. He wants to have supper with us. Our prayer should be like having snack food in front of the fireplace with Jesus.

There will be times when we want to spend hours with Him, but what about in-between meal snacks.

Sinkers on the line

God says that we can test Him in prayer. If we are willing to throw out big prayers, He is willing to answer them. We need only pray into His will. Sometimes, we put our own sinkers on our line to God. We curse the prayers without knowing because we don't believe that God is actually listening.

When I was praying for my daughter who was on drugs, I prayed 90 chapters of the book of Psalms. Often, I felt that I was talking to myself instead of God. He showed me that He was present the whole time by giving me a vision. While in the desert, He showed me, my daughter, at the foot of the cross with her head bowed, too embarrassed to come to Him for her healing. I knew that when she looked at His face, she would be healed. So, I prayed for this to be so. But, I confess, I didn't really believe in the vision, because I had never prayed into a vision before.

Within two weeks my daughter showed up in the church with everything she owned. That night, she knelt on the porch of our house and prayed for God to give her the same hunger for Him that she had for drugs. Three days later, she checked herself into a drug a rehabilitation center. She was healed through prayer.

But, God dealt with me. After she came home, I played a song that I had prayed for her. When the music started, she came down the stairs and dropped to her knees on the carpet in the middle of the sunken living room.

At first, she wept, just like the vision I had seen in the desert. She hung her head. And, at that time, God put a light on her. It was like He shone a spotlight on her for me to look. As the song progressed, she started to praise Him. When she did, she raised her head and looked into His face. I could see it. Oh, how special I felt to be part of this most special time of her life!

And, I realized that I hadn't believed Him for the message that He had given me in the desert. I had prayed out of obedience, not out of faith. But, still, He had answered my request and brought my daughter back to me. So, I, too, dropped to my knees and thanked the Savior who saved us both.

Start at the Beginning

Prayer needs to be met at the point of entry for the problem. We can pray around and around, but until we go through the gate, we will not gain entrance into the city. We have to find the key to the door. All the keys have been given to us! Jesus has entrusted to us the keys the Kingdom of Heaven. We need to learn how to use them.

Sometimes we are standing in the way of the answer. We need to reach out for it but don't know how. We may be praying one direction when God wants to answer a totally different direction.

I have a friend whose daughter 'borrowed' his Jeep and went on an excursion with her friends. She told him that she was going to the mall, but went to the desert 4 wheeling. The girls rolled the Jeep, and demolished it.

My friend called me right away and asked me to pray. The response that I got from God, when I asked Him about it was, "I am about to move him up. This is not a disaster, but a promotion."

I told my friend what God had told me. He was skeptical, but trusted and prayed into what I told him.

It took a little time, but my friend is now driving a brand new car, has lost weight (because he had to walk for a while) and his daughter has a new attitude about driving.

And, it didn't cost my friend any financial loss. God provides for His plans.

God wants to bring light into our darkness. He doesn't want our prayer closet to be dark. He wants us to know how to get the answers to our prayers. He has provided Wisdom; His thoughts, for us.

We don't need to tackle the problem on our own. He is available to help us. No matter how diligent and disciplined we are, if we do not pray into His will, we will not be successful.

God is good. He wants nothing more than for His children to call to Him and to respond.

Love Flow, Overflow

Seek to go
to the place of God's
joy where God moves your heart;
Where He fills it with His love, up to, overflowing.
For, joy doesn't flow, it overflows because it's from a heart
filled from the inside. It bubbles up and over like seltzer water.

Longing and Desire

The woman longs for her husband who is away. He is on
a fishing trip. But, her desire must not be for herself.
For, if He returns early, perhaps, there will
be a shortage of fish caught. As we long
for the return of Christ, our desire
is
for the fisherman to bring home
all the fish He can catch.

God Wakes us
You would not get
up unless I woke you. I will
be your uprising.

22 Galleons
22 Galleons sail
into the harbor in the morning
at high tide. There is a rate of turn. It has
to do with turn radius. More prayer = a bigger keel.
The more that prayer is extended into the presence
of the water, the faster that big ship will turn.

Fishing with the Father

Joy and delight in fellowship with the Father. It's a Father,
Son fishing trip. We have the gear and He untangles the line.
When we go overboard, He sends a life ring after us because
we are supposed to be fishing, but we don't pay attention.
We were noisy and scared the fish. We don't know when
to start and stop our conversations with others. And, we
don't know how to use the net when they get close.
We think we can use our bare hands. Then, we cry
and mope when the unsaved slip through our
fingers like a slippery fish. Let Me show you
how to use the net. Gentle. You must
extend
yourself for them. Reach out.
Be moved by My Holy Spirit
to do what I need. For
even though, I
trained as a
carpenter,
I still
know
To
fish.
I caught
You didn't
I? Hook, line and
sinker you followed Me to
the depths of My love and won't
let go. It's in the bate and how you
string the line. Throw Me the line, let Me
bait your hook. I know what I'm doing, I'm the
fisherman. Your line has the buoy, Mine the hook.
Use Mine. We need to use His line. We do not know
how much weight to put on ours. We must wait on Him

Holy Spirit Direction

We need to learn how to pray into His will. When we are filled with the Holy Spirit and allow His Word to speak through us, then, we will become the breath of God.

The breath of God is what moves things. The Holy Spirit will be happy to provide direction to us if we let Him. We need to create an environment that He can operate in. Solomon did it when he dedicated the temple. Read his words:

Now arise, O Lord and come to your resting place, you and the ark of your might. May your priests be clothed with salvation, and may your saints rejoice in Your goodness.

The Elements that made Solomon Right.

There are elements that make our heart a place where God wants to hang out. We want to become His hanger.

Willingness: We need to be open to be willing to do what ever He wants us to do.

Song of Praise in our heart: We need to have an attitude of praise in our heart toward Him. It is for His Glory that we pray, not our own.

Pursue Holiness: Holiness is the end product of our lives here on earth. We can have holiness on earth, but not without some pursuit of it.

Purity: Keep ourselves unstained from the world. We need to seek to do God's will, alone, apart from others.

Openness: Be open to new ideas from God.

Broken: Be separated. Allow God to speak to our Spirit, and our spirit to our soul and our soul to our flesh. Then our flesh will do what our spirit needs to do to be in line with the Spirit of God.

Easily moved: We need to become easily moved. Not firmly fixed on our own ideas.

Listen: Open our spiritual eyes and ears to see and hear what He has for us.

Obedient: Be obedient to do whatever He tells us to do.

The goal is to pray into the purposes and character of God. It is revealed in Scripture, words of God in prophecy, dreams, visions, voice of God, and revelations in His creation. We seek guidance from the Holy Spirit. It is to be alone and in unity with others. God will speak back to us

We pray the way God tells us to. He is looking for those who petition: When Daniel learned of the bad news toward the kingdom, He went up and prayed openly on His porch because he knew it was the right thing to do. His heart was in tune with God's heart and ideas for the kingdom.

We need to become those who pray because it is the right thing to do, not because of any rules men make. Pray openly to God in the right direction, and on our knees. He continued doing something that God had told him to do. He went in the same direction until God said to turn.

II Chronicles 6:41, Psalms 18, Daniel 6:11

Keys

Tantamount to your experience is the unsheathing of Excalibur. Learning to uncover the enemy, take his keys and put them into your pocket. By the Spirit of God you walk straight into his kingdom and by the authority given to you as a child of God, you pick up your keys from inside his door. They are yours. Go get them.

Life and Mercy River

The river increases with unification. The Life and Mercy River flows when there's a joining of reason with the blood of the Lamb. Be wrapped. Be held. Be stilled.

(The unsheathing of the sword of Satan is explained in a book called Katishá. Glorybound Publishing. It is a book of the tricks of the enemy and how to combat them in prayer.)

Perspective to the Goal

When we look toward the goal, we need to
ask God to give us the perspective to it.
If our vision is not clear, then we
will have no clear reference to it.
If we do not know where the net is,
we can not be expected to get the ball
over it during a serve. God wants
us to serve Him in every
aspect of our
lives all
along
the
way.
We need
to ask
Him
to
provide
clear perspective
for us as we move along
the path that He lays out for us.

Wrong Attitudes we Bring to Prayer

Being too Casual before God.

We need to seek relationship with God as a child who is in need of a mediator. We are sinners and He has paid the ransom to remove our feet from the shackles.

Remember, we are considered enemies of God when we are without repentance. We should never think we can come casually into the presence of God. He honors our reverence toward Him. (Job 33:26)

An attitude against the person we are praying for:

Moses was a chosen leader by God, so He had the authority to speak for the people. He had to put himself completely into God's hands to be used to lead the people.

In the story, the people grew impatient and spoke against God and against Moses. Then, the Lord sent venomous snakes among them.

Then, they came to Moses and said, "We have sinned when we spoke against you and God. Pray that the Lord will take the snakes away."

So Moses prayed for the people. Then the Lord told him what to do. He made a bronze snake. Put it on a pole and had the people look at it. They were healed. (Numbers 21:4-9)

He had to put his own attitudes aside. Then, he entreated God for them. He waited for instructions from God, then, believed the answer God had given him. He went forward to act on what God told him to do. He spent his energy for another who had wronged him: he sacrificed Himself for their needs, even though they talked bad about him.

He conveyed the message to the people so they would be healed. They had to look to the healer.

When God Comes to you with a Problem:

In Deuteronomy 9:14 God told Moses that the people had become corrupt, turned away from what He had commanded them and cast an idol for themselves. He says, "Let me alone, so that I may destroy them, and blot out their name...and make a nation of you."

This time: God tells him there is a problem. Moses goes to the people first and attempts to talk with them. He tried to fix things but only became angry, resulting in broken tablets.

Notice that he does what God tells him to do. He burns the calf in the fire, crushes it up, and puts it in the stream that flows to the people. Then, Moses turned to God in prayer, making himself prostrate and fasting for 40 days because He feared the anger and wrath of the Lord. He prays a special prayer for Aaron, his brother, who was supposed to be in charge of them at this time when they were disobedient.

He knew there was a problem. And, he knew how mad God was.... mad enough to change the whole plan and not include them in any of it.

An interesting conversation between God and Moses occurs when God asks him not to pray for the people. I asked Him why He would ask Moses not to pray?

God asked him not to pray because He knew that Moses could change His mind. He knew that if Moses prayed, He would be gracious and forgive the people....and He did.

God may tell you of a problem that needs to be fixed. The proper response isn't to go fix it. You will mess it up more.

Moses became angry. Because He was angry, He did not avoid God, but spent time in fasting to try to get his flesh out of the middle of the situation. Then, He entreated God, and God told him what to do. The results of the sin still flowed to the people, but God's wrath stayed. God forgave Moses' anger and told him how to replace what was broken.

Prayer from the heart is blessed

Hannah is a good example of praying from her heart when she prayed for the baby Samuel. She went to where God was. She goes to the temple and cries out to Him with the bitterness of her soul. She was weeping on the steps openly crying to Him to meet her needs for a child.

She made a deal with God If He gave the child to her, she would give him back to God. (God makes deals). Then, she kept on praying. She was persistent when she poured out her soul to the Lord. God used Eli to bless her prayer into action.

Hannah met God where she was. She was in an anguished state. She went to where He was, she didn't try to bring Him to her. She went to the Temple. She poured out her heart to Him and He responded to her prayer with an answer brought through Eli.

Then, when God answered her prayers, she kept her promise, sending Samuel back to the temple. (I Samuel 1)

Prodding Sheep

Everlasting, Omnipotent Savior why do you chide Your people? You nudge the sheep, prodding them gently. Otherwise they will continue to walk along the fence to look for a way out. Then, they focus on the fence instead of My hand that will direct them the way out.

God's Antenna

The dream:

There is a man with large television antennas tied to himself all over. These are the antennas that are used on top of houses. He looks ridiculous. 'Sit in God's presence and display His love to others.'

Interpretation:

He has provided guidance systems for us, but we need to turn on our radar system. Put up our antenna.

We need to tune our receiver to God's channel. He has a 24-hour network channel that He is televising over to us. When we sit in His presence, we get on His channel. We tune into what He is all about.

We receive Jesus Christ as our Lord and Savior when we ask Him to cleanse us of our sins. He does it. But we must continue to receive Him; to receive His words to us.

It's like marrying someone, then never speaking to him, when we stop being open to receiving the words of Jesus day after day. He wants to have a relationship with us: one of communication. The Spirit of Truth will guide us into all truth and only speak what He hears from the Father.

There are no signals from God apart from Him sending them to us. We cannot find Him on our own. Our antennas aren't big enough to catch His signals.

God wants us to receive His words as they actually are, the word from Him, not as the word of men, and allow it to work in us. The words of God are active and work in us to change our lives. When we listen and obey, God will honor us by trusting us with more. There is an inheritance waiting for us as we walk into His words with obedience to them.

Proverbs 19:20, Matthew 7.8, 10.8, Luke 8.13,9, John 1,16, Romans 1.5, 5.11, Galatians 4.5, James 1.21, 1 Peter 1.9, 5.4.

Reception Repair

*Delight, determine, desire. Because I delight in
you, what I determine for you, will be your desire.
Because I know you, I know your desire, your delight,
your heart. While you're listening, listen to your own heart,*
please. We have turned it off like a television set. We became
discouraged because we thought it was broke when we could
only pick up one channel. We figured it was either a problem
with the set; us, or the reception; God is gone. We forgot to
check the antenna. We must be open to receive all that He
has for us. Our heart is the reception and the channel.
We can't change it, He does. When we become
receptive, He doesn't make new TV
stations for us, He just increases
our reception of the only
one He is on. There's
a lot of satellites
out there
we have
never picked up
on. We need to tune-up.
Listen. Tune into the station
He has for us. Let Him help to find
that station. He does reception repair. He makes
house calls. Call Him. Then answer. Be open, connect.

Coming Through Closed Doors

Walls. Sometimes we think that a door is locked, or we have a wall in front of us. Actually, we are looking at the ceiling, not the wall. We reach the wall when we go as far as our vision can take us. Then, we need to cash it in for a new vision.

In the Bible, Christians are compared to trees. We grow being watered by God and are planted together in clumps, like forests.

Pillars are made of the center cut of trees, and I noticed that it is pillars that hold up the ceiling of most buildings. Jesus tells Peter, at one time, that he is a pillar of the Church and that the structure of the Church will be founded on him.

Later, in the book of Revelation, the rest of us are called pillars. I believe Jesus is talking about how we are to uphold the structure and vision of the building of the Church.

But, sometimes, I have noticed that people are unhappy in positions within the Church. They want to sing, but there is no room in the Choir. Or, they want to preach, but the pulpit is full. They become discouraged after waiting several years for an opportunity to minister within the gifts that God has blessed them in, so they leave and find another Church. It is as if they hit a wall and cannot find the door that needs to be open for them do what they know God wants them to do.

So, what has happened?
The pillars hold up the Church. If a pillar is in one of the adjacent rooms and needs to be moved, then it must be turned sideways and carried into the main sanctuary to be stood upright again. We have to lay down our vision for the Church to be movable into the main sanctuary. The Church pillars hold up the vision. If the pillar is too short, it is of no use to the building. The pillar is made of the core of the tree.

The center cut needs to be vertical to have maximum strength and use. Maybe we think we are a cross member and God really wants to use us as a pillar. If we hang onto the things of the past and try to mix them with God's new vision, it doesn't work. We will feel like we have hit a wall. His vision will be the largest vision we can have. What are the needs for us that God sees? He looks from the top down.

We must tear the ceiling off our vision and allow God to impart to us and put His ceiling on it. If we reach a wall, what do we do? Look for the door first. If it is locked, then put ourselves down (humble ourselves and place our visions at His feet).

We have already been given the keys, so search ourselves and our purses. What have we brought with us that is holding us back? If there is no door, then turn aside, not back. God longs to move us with His hands, not heavy equipment.

The master-builder has the plans for His Church and knows where the columns need to be placed. They are all based on the foundation in Him and the revelation of His Word to the individual.

Following the wrong vision will lead us to max out on our resources, and when they stop, and our vision continues, there will not be a closed-door, but a wall without a door, a ceiling.

How do you know? Check your alignment with Him.

Walking into the Sea

We can walk into the sea when it becomes dry ground as it did
for the Children of Israel as they left Egypt to escape slavery.
The same is true for us, today. We can learn about God
and become part of the miracles when we learn
how to part the sea and walk on dry ground as they
did. We don't have to learn to walk on the ocean, for He
parts the sea for us. We walk where He tells us to go. And
when we do, we will land where we are supposed to be. Just
like a cat when you toss it up in the air; amazing. Every
time he will land on his feet. Even a kitten. Amazing
Who taught them to do that? A dog won't.
You toss him up and he comes down
crooked and panicked.
It's not to say
that the kitten
isn't worried.
We are
like the
kitten.
Fly
on
the
wind of His words, released by His hand.
His
voice
sustains
us. Carries us up
and down. That's the elevator.
Up and down. We are to go up and
down with the octaves of His voice. He is the
song into our soul. Isn't it amazing how that cat
always lands on its feet. Upright. O to be like that puddy
cat. To be continuously upright even when I'm in mid air

Life or Liberty

Which is more important. Life or liberty. I would
hate to choose. Thank you, Jesus You have given
both. New life, new freedom. It's like a road we
come across after wandering through the trees. It's
not new, but new to us because we only just now
found it. So, we merge with that road. It's one way.
From behind to ahead. Eternity past to God only knows.
But, we've merged. We weren't really on a marked
trail. We had forged our own way through the bramble.
We marched out from our place and then felt obligated
to continue our way. Our own way. We just grabbed a
machete and hacked away at anything stopping us. We
had to get through. We had a goal, a destination.
But the goals kept changing. With new places
we saw over the next horizon.
Yet, we never
reached
where
we wanted
to go. No, Thank you Jesus, we haven't.
Those goals wouldn't
have made us
truly happy. He
knows
that the
only true
happiness
is in life and
freedom and His road
is the only one that goes there.

Air Out

Dream:

There's a man who is connected to three types of chest tube drainages. All of them have a water seal. All are immersed in the water.

He's always better if you can make him breathe with his diaphragm because there are three types of chest tube drainages. All are connected to the lungs. The last container is full of infection type sludge. It can cause death. We need to open the bag and air it out. There's a plastic bag covering the infection of sludge in the last container.

Interpretation:

We have three types of ways we can air out our heart issues. We can tell others, we can tell God, or we can tell ourselves. When we talk to ourselves, we just full up with sludge. We become a container full of the infection process. We can cover it up, but God says that we only are using see-thru plastic bags, and everyone knows that we need airing. We need to open that bag; that area that we insist on only talking to ourselves about, to Him.

When Jesus was stabbed, there flowed out water and blood. We need to let His blood and the water and presence of God flow through us. We need to give up the rest to Him. Air out anything that stands between us and airing out His sacrifice through our lives and allowing His presence to flow through.

Through the Building

The Dream:

My husband, Paul, has something to do where He goes through the center of the building. It's in the middle of the city. It's is raining outside, so I offer to drive around the block to pick him up on the other side of the building. He will go in one side of the building and come out in another place on a different street. He will go in on the south side and come out on the west side. I pass by a newsstand.

When I get into the vehicle, it is a tan SUV. There are people already in there. It is a family of black people. They are big. There is a father, mother, and daughter. I wonder if there will be enough room for Paul, but they assure me that they will move over to make room for him. When I turn around, all three are smashed into the back seat. It's tight, but they fit because they want to. They are nice.

The streets are one way, so I drive around. I have time, so I take an extra loop. I go around a second block. When I get to the bottom of a block, there is a barricade. The road ends at a large empty lot next to the sea. I am not paying attention, so I barrel right through it. It is not really any problem to my vehicle because it is an ATV. We go over the rocks and down into the lot. I don't mind the ride. It's no big deal. I circle the lot, admiring the sea, and get back to what I was supposed to do, picking up Paul.

I come around the corner, and He is waiting. He is mad because my passengers have turned off the GPS. There was one on the dashboard. He wanted to see where He was going.

Interpretation:

My husband, like Jesus, wants to go through the center of the building process with the Church. He is reigning. He is pouring out His power, His love, His reign on all. There is news on the street of His reign. He wants us to get into A TV. He wants our vehicle to be by His vision. He provides all-terrain vision for us; in all weather, all conditions; all the time.

Mine has others already waiting for me. A large family. They are not what I expected, but they are nice. They have been waiting for me to get into the vehicle. They are willing to do whatever it takes to be along for the ride; to ride in that All-Terrain Vehicle. To ride within the vision that God has for them. When I tell them that they must make a place for the Husband, they are quick to take the back seat.

There were some blocks. I only needed to go around one, but I was enjoying the ride, so, I took out two. In fact, by my testing in what God has for me, I took out the barricade. I have gotten into the vision that God has provided and He has placed the wheel in my fingers and driven me straight over the rocks (revelational knowledge of Him) and into a flat spot near the sea. He has brought me to a place of being able to see. It is a flat spot without fear of the enemy.

When we rest in what God has for us, He will take us through the barricades without a problem. In fact, He will take others with us as well. Trust him.

When the husband gets inside the car, He is mad because they have turned off the GPS. It is a system that tells us where we are in relation to the satellites. God wants to be our mobile Global Positioning System. Don't turn Him off. His information system is like the one embedded in the dashboard. It needs to be on and in front of us to lead us.

Envision a Miracle

Because when you envision it, the antennae
on the rooftop is turned to pick up signals
from God. Pick them up. See them.
Follow the signs to the destination.
Why did we think we could get there
without signs? We can't. That is why it
is a rare gift. People have to be able to
see the signs. Have open eyes and ears to
God. His vision. Ship to shore, anchor
the boat. We are supposed to
anchor
the
boat and walk to shore.
We have been
thinking
that
we drive
the boat to shore.
No wonder we run aground so often.
Teach us to walk on water, O Lord!

Walk into the Steps

Walk into the steps. Go toward.

Interpretation

When we pray into the will of God, then we can pray with faith that it will happen. If we ask God what His will is, then pray 'into' that perfect will, then we are guaranteed victory. We need to walk toward Him. He is calling out to us.

When we ask Him something, we need to wait on Him for the answer. Then, have a pad and pen ready to copy it. Sometimes it will not make sense right then. But, we can always take it back to Him again and again for clarification. He will be true to answer us.

Also, maybe He doesn't want to reveal all of the steps in the process at this time for what He is doing. He wants us to step out in faith with the information that He gives us. He wants us to go toward the answer.

Sometimes, when He gives an answer, it is not the final answer. There are several steps in-between that must be done first to get there. He may be sending us in a specific direction for another purpose. Perhaps He tells us to go to a Church meeting at a different Church. At first, He tells the purpose. Then, when we go, we learn that there are several other purposes for us being there. He just needed to get us there in the first place. We simply need to start walking.

Paper Patterns

The dream:

I was going through some old things and found a pattern book with patterns for little dolls and furniture. They were paper patterns. A guy offered to buy it from me. I gave it to him. I asked him why He wanted it. He says it is because it is hard to find patterns of things that fit together like the dolls that fit on the furniture.

Interpretation:

I have been going through the Bible and God has revealed to me patterns for living. He has shown how it fits together to live within the Kingdom of God. It is like dolls with their furniture and clothes. He provides the house and has provided us the patterns for how to sit within His Kingdom. He gives us what, where, and how. The provisions of God are for those who value them.

Combination

Ask Him for the combination that releases the blessings in your life. He is the one who holds the keys. Maybe you are looking for the wrong type of key. Maybe it is a safety box filled with precious jewels and secret documents and titles to lands yet unclaimed.

The Rescue

The rescue of God breaks through. His brokenness breaks through our brokenness in a place that only exists in the mind of God. Faith

Interpretation:

He tells us to 'Go' Take no provisions. Only a walking stick. We are to take only ourselves and the staff of life; the God/Angelic stuff. We pour out ourselves to Him. Then He pours Himself into those we minister to, as we respond to Him. It is like He becomes 'them' to us. He says that if we give a child a cup of water in His name, it is as if we have given him a glass of water. If we have done it to the least of His children, we have done it for Him.

Give to God in the presence of the other person

Power flows from negative to positive for the glory of God to the unity of His presence through us.

The Door can't open when we are standing in front of the elevator door.
We need to move out of the way for God to speak to His children Himself.

Two Way Glass

Be a glass house. You provide the frame,
I'll provide the windows.
Glorious windows to heaven, from heaven.
Not one way glass. It's two way glass.
We both see through to each other.

The Wall:
Where Presence and Kingdom Meet

The dream:

A Christian Brother gives me two pictures. I am standing on an upper wall in front of a church structure. The wall is very tall; about 60 feet. I am at the very top of it, looking forward to balancing on the wall. I am surprised at how tall the wall is.

Then, He shows me another picture. It is the same City behind the wall, but in this picture, it shows a second wall, that is lower. There is a woman standing on that wall too. She looks like she could be me, as well.

In both pictures, the women are facing outward from the city, looking for something. They don't seem to notice that they are on top of a wall that is narrow.

Interpretation:

In the dream, I am standing on a wall with an ancient city behind. It is the City of the Kingdom of God. Often, the Church is regarded as a 'wall' that God is building. In the New Testament, He talks about us being stones in the wall of the building. We are part of the building process. We are as part of the wall itself.

When we learn our position within the Kingdom of God (the Ancient City), then we will know where to stand.

In the dream, I am standing on the wall. A wall can also be a structure built of stones. Jesus is the cornerstone and the capstone. It symbolizes the start and stops of all that Jesus is: His salvation package for us. When we stand on the wall, it means that we are standing on the 'Salvation package' that Jesus has given to us. We are essentially, standing on the promises of the building of His Kingdom with Jesus as King.

When we become Children of God, we can stand on all that He has given. We stand firm on these promises, even though sometimes it may look to others like we will fall, we won't.

There are others that are standing on the promises and looking for God to come; to bring His will to his Kingdom. No matter how small the promises we are standing on, we can look for His presence to meet His Kingdom. Just because we don't know a lot of scripture, we can still stand on whatever we know. All of the promises are true, so no matter which ones we claim, all of them are true.

The reason that we look to God is to see things change. We are looking for His hand to move within our world to bring change. He has given us the power to pray in His Kingdom. He has placed the keys to the Heavenly Kingdom in our hands. It is through prayer.

We have a unique position between two kingdoms. We live here, yet we belong to another. When we have a need in prayer, we can ask God to bring His Kingdom. We live in a 'default' world. This Kingdom is run by 'the prince of the power of the Air, Satan'. Without the intervention of God, there is pain, suffering, loss, and separation from Him. When He comes to help us, He brings relief from our problems; life and peace, joy and strength, hope for our despair.

We can ask for hope because God promises hope to His children. In essence, we stand upon the promises of God and look for His salvation to come to us in our time of need. When God shows up, He does not send His helpers to do His will.

No, He comes Himself. He comes because He is the Father. Just like when a child has fallen in the park and calls out to her father for rescue, God will come Himself to our rescue when we call out to Him

We represent the Kingdom of God between two worlds. Our back is to the Kingdom of God. He backs us. Our front is to this world. When we pray from a position of standing on the Word of God is like we are on top of a wall. From this position, we can see the presence of God coming to help those in need. When His presence comes, then His will is done and His Kingdom comes. They are inseparable.

Matthew 6:9,16:19,19:14, John 14:2,18:36, Ephesians 2.

Dedication of a Day

Father, I dedicate this
day to You. Make me new. I don't
like who I was yesterday. It's not that I
was bad. It's just that I know I wasn't as good
as I need to be. So, Dear Lord, create Your newness
within me. Revive my soul, refresh my spirit. Light the
lamp of the knowledge of You within my heart. I let go of my
way. I release my fingers of what I cling to and ask for You
to put them into Your will for me. Give me grace for the
time when I feel that emptiness while my fingers are
open from letting go and when You fill me with
what I need. Bridge my uneasiness
with the gift of faith,
I pray,
dear Lord. Faith to
believe You for Your promises.
For, in thee, do I put my trust. I love You.

Deliverance comes when He presses a heart that
is willing through the place where it was meant to go.
It is like a peg that a child pounds through a board. Push
the water and it will part. Then, you will see your dry ground.

Christen the Ship

Now is the time to christen the ship. Break wine
across the bow. My presence to cross over
the covenant whereby I will bring My Spirit
of Counsel, Wisdom, Might, Understanding,
Knowledge, and truth by way of My Presence.
Christen My presence among My people. For
you have assured Me of the covenants. Thank
You for helping Me to build a seaworthy vessel;
one that holds My heart's desire designed to bring
the blessings of My Mercy and Grace to My Kids.
It is a boat that comes with nets to catch other fish,
As well. More kids will be brought into the boat
when you float it. Go ahead, let go, let it slide down
the rails and be gently lowered into My hands,
My face, My Presence. You see, it is where
My Presence within you meets My
Presence in a vessel That I send,
You on the mission I have
planned for you since the
beginning of time. The
two presences
collide
and
there will be like
a clap of thunder.
A mighty sound
It will make
as the angels
shout when
the vessel
connects
to the surface
that it is meant to float in.
A mighty work for Me has been finished.
Congratulations, well done good and faithful servant.

Revival and Revolution

What difference is there between light and life?
Debt and death? Understanding and intuition?
Revival and revolution?
With light, you can see where you are going.
With life, you can get there. Debt is
what is due to God from us because of
our position. Our final payment is death.
Death to the dream, death to our ideas, death to us.
Through the Holy Spirit, we have not merely intuition,
but an understanding of God's Word, will and ways.
Of how Jesus is the light came to pay our debt,
give us life in exchange for death and
insure understanding of the
Kingdom of God.
As we move
From
The
feeling
of intuition into
assurance, then we step from
'I think so' into faith. Our 'maybe'
becomes our 'yes' through Him.
He will sustain His 'yes'. That's when
we will find ourselves amidst a revolution.

Baptism

Baptism is for the weak willed.
You go in one way
and come out another.
Go down weighed with sin and come up cleaned.
Baptism is a demonstration of dependency.
A public show of weak knees going down.
Face to face with the purity of our Lord.
Taking all He has for us, being washed,
cleansed, refreshed, made new.
The Christian life is lived through the weak kneed.
Those dependent ones.
And you thought it was about getting wet.

Writing Index

God Wakes Us	227		Life and Mercy River	231
God's Antenna	236		Life or Liberty	242
God's Oreo Sandwich	198		Light Bright	125
Gold Dust	185		Longing and Desire	227
Golden Heart	214		Lost Sheep	70
Grace Flies Down	176		Love Flow, Overflow	227
Greater Purpose	13		Luke Warm	114
Healing	164		Manna	193
Healing of the Nations	68		Ministry	29
Healing on His Wings	165		Mobile Cleansing Team	92
Hearing Clearly	126		Mysterious Diner	170
Heart Service	121		No Met Yes	41
Heart Surgery	56		No Worry	101
Hi Jacked Word	179		Open Heart	168
Hidden Head Lights	157		Open Heavens	27
Hiding with Dog Food	205		Opening the Gifts	78
His Desire	39		Other's Sinfulness	181
His Son	22		Our Pond	216
Holy Spirit Direction	229		Our Spirit	122
Hop in Circles	177		Our Uniform	72
Hum	113		Pacer	187
Hummingbird	142		Paddy Cake	191
Hungry	72		Paper Patterns	247
Ideopathic Telepathic	180		Parquet	181
Important Jobs	85		Paw Prints	121
In Tune	49		Perspective to the Goal	232
Indwells	94		Pitter Patter	98
Inspire God	77		Porch Light	42
Joy and Delight	112		Power in our Voice	171
Judgment and Mercy	123		Prayer for Bread	113
Just Believing	82		Prayer Rainbow	220
Keys	231		Pre Paired Union	93
Kisses of Wisdom	100		Presence in Church	102
Kitchen Utensil	126		Presence with Gifts	109
Knowledge of Me	94		Problems in Prayer	221
Lemon Aid	204		Prodding Sheep	235
Lemon Delight	90		Prophecy	133

About the Author

Sheri Hauser grew up in Seattle, Washington accustomed to the rainy days and nights going on long hikes in the Cascades in the summer and snow skiing in the winter. She graduated from High School in Leavenworth, Washington and attended Bible College in Oregon. Married at 20, she went on to nursing school and had two children. In 2001, she began writing spiritual books and started to look for a publisher. Not finding one who would accept her manuscript, she opted to learn what was needed to grow her own publishing company. Initially the company was called Glory Bound Books and obtained license in Las Vegas in 2005. As the company grew, she tossed her entire nursing paycheck into purchasing printers and software. She attended classes at the University of Las Vegas for graphic design, web site development and photo shop. It took three years of intensive study to learn papers, the publishing industry and how to put books together. Throughout this time, she developed the Lasertrain (a set of digital templates for making your own books). She climbed the ladder of her profession and after 30 years as a Cardiothoracic Nurse in Intensive Care, she retired from nursing full-time to dedicate her time to grow a publishing company. By 2016, she had written 25 books, and published over 600 books (from authors).

Her and her husband relocated to Camp Verde, Arizona in 2017 and set the publishing company in an old house living in the upstairs. They love the quiet cowboy town and she is presently active in forming a newly developing Chamber of Commerce. She is the president.

Additionally, she is part of the Curriculum Development Team and a Facilitator teaching classes related to publishing at Osher Life Long Learning Institute.

2020 started off with a bang when she began doing ads on Amazon for her books. Today, she has 15 books on page 1 of their topic search engines and is actively seeing sales daily.

Sheri Hauser is the author of several series of books including: Glorybound Lasertrain, Dream Books with Steps to Intimacy with God, GBK Children's books and text books on publishing.

Sheri's Books

The manuals are books which help prepare for the release of the prophetic wave of the Holy Spirit as spoken of in Joel 2. These books are written from dreams. The dreams were given over a period of around 6 months or so. As they were received, I carefully interpreted them using Scriptures. Then I was given an outline dream. The dreams of the specific subject were then put into the outline. That forms the books. There are 21 books. Initially, all of the books were as one giant book. Then as I received more dreams of direction, the books began to split; first into four, then into more (like bread rising in a bowl) they grew over time within the right environment. The first book split into what became the first four books. I was instructed to turn over the stack and release them. So, I released Coriantá, having it professionally edited and printed at the cost of $37,000. By the time I got to the next book, I realized that the books were reproducing at an alarming rate, and I would never have enough money to print them conventionally, so I asked God if I could have a publishing company.

He said, "Sure."

I quickly responded, "I don't know anything about a publishing company."

His response, "That's OK. It will come in a box with instructions."

I quickly called the guy who put together my first book and then ordered the computer program which he specified as the one for making books. Guess what? It came in a box with instructions. (Smile). Several of the books sprouted due to the response from individuals asking questions--such as *Simple Fun Christian Dream*

Interpretation, the three books in the Prophetic Prayer Series as well as *Prophetic Interpretation of Art*.

All of the books are available as e-books and bound copies regular and large print through Amazon.com. Printed bound, signed, color editions are available directly through Glorybound Publishing. Use the contact page on the web site to order.

The Prophetic Wave

Manuals for a Prophetic Wave of the Holy Spirit with Miracles, Signs and Wonders

And Afterwards I will Pour Out My Spirit
Christian Authors Driving the Market
Dream Language Understood
Faith on a Wing and a Prayer
Filled with the Holy Spirit
Foundational Prophetic Prayer
Going to the Center of God's Heart
Growing Ministry to Seed instead of Fruit
Inspirational 3-D Poetry
Intimate Relationship with Jesus
Leading Prophetic Prayer
Living in the Haunted House of my Head
Living in the Shadow of the Sins of our Parents
Personal Prophetic Prayer
Preparing the Bride of Christ: Allegorical
Prophetic Interpretation of Art
Sharing Prophetic Gifts in the Church
Simple Fun Christian Dream Interpretation
Spiritual Authority Over Demon Dragons
Tactical Demonic Warfare
Why the Glory Departed

Made in the USA
Middletown, DE
26 January 2021